The Quotable Teacher

Books by Randy Howe

Flags of the Fifty States and Their Incredible Histories

The Quotable Teacher

Edited by
Randy Howe

THE LYONS PRESS
Guilford, Connecticut
An imprint of The Globe Pequot Press

To Yolanda DeStefano

The Lyons Press is an imprint of The Globe Pequot Press.

10 9 8 7 6 5 4 3 2

ISBN 1-58574-659-2

Printed in the United States of America

Library of Congress Cataloging-in-Publication data is available on file.

There is no real teacher who in practice
does not believe in the existence of the soul,
or in a magic that acts on it through speech.

ALLAN BLOOM (1930–1992)

The wisdom of the wise
and the experience of the ages
are perpetuated in quotations.

BENJAMIN DISRAELI (1804–1881)

Contents

Acknowledgments

For all their support, a debt of gratitude to Alicia Solís, Ann Treistman, and Greg MacGilpin.

Introduction

Every morning, hundreds of thousands of people get up to face the most demanding critics you could ever hope to know. Anyone who has ever stood before a classroom full of students understands why.

Teaching is an art form that combines the intellectual with the spiritual, the philosophic with the philanthropic. Look into the heart of good teaching and you will find love. On "Abbey Road," The Beatles sing of the symbiotic nature of love: that in the end, the beautifully balanced nature of give and take will reveal itself. The classroom should be just such a place—with the students learning from the teacher just as the teacher is learning from the students.

When a teacher has found the balance between philosophy and philanthropy, pedagogy and inspiration, discipline and nurture, the future begins to look brighter. Educators who are passionate about their work reflect the thoughts of Robert Frost who writes of uniting "my vocation with my avocation/as my two eyes join in sight," in "Two Tramps in Mud Time." "Only where love and need are one," Frost continues, "And the work is play for mortal stakes/Is the deed ever really done/For Heaven and for future's sake."

As a new teacher, the future didn't look particularly bright. I meant well, but struggled to find my stride. Experience brought with it some degree of knowledge and teaching style and nowadays I can bring proper closure to a lesson; I am capable of disciplining a student without burning a bridge; I am comfortable assessing student performance with formal and informal measures; I can deal with an irate parent without becoming irate myself. There may be areas that still beg for improvement, but more and more often I am able to strike the balance that brings the joy of learning to both me and my students. Over the course of this learning, my vocation has become my avocation; my profession, my passion.

I did my social studies student teaching in a seventh grade classroom in western New York: I learned that Seneca Falls was a hotbed for the feminist movement and that there really are parents who allow their kids to miss school for the first day of hunting season.

I taught all four academic subjects in a program for teen mothers: over the course of seven years I learned how hard it is to balance goals and parenthood. I also learned all about unconditional love and the tricks of the diaper changing trade.

I taught night school to people twice my age: I learned how a GED diploma can mean the difference between earning minimum wage and getting off welfare. It is the difference between shame and pride.

I attended the Summer Law Institute at Columbia University and learned that education has become very litigious (everything from locker searches to bussing to the things teachers do in the privacy of their own home to the things students do while at a party), that the country's Hispanic population recently surpassed the African-American population, and that one of my professors, although brilliant, is just another optimistically disgruntled Red Sox fan.

I spent a year as the administrator for a culinary arts program: I learned that vocational interests can become professional passions with the proper guidance and instruction. I also learned to visit the baking class every Wednesday morning for cinnamon rolls!

And just recently I made the switch from high school to elementary school to be a special education teacher in New Haven: I am back to learning my ABCs and 123s. I *have* to if I am to teach them to others.

What have I learned as a result of all this? That I could teach in just about any school, at just about any level, and be happy.

Compiling *The Quotable Teacher* was like one big teachable moment for me. Each new quote lent the words to describe so many of my unspoken thoughts and emotions. I was able to synthesize all of my experiences into one meaningful experience and it quickly became obvious that we learn not only from the teachings of others, but from our own teaching as well. This is something I have been learning ever since the day I first set foot in the classroom as "Mr. Howe."

I started teaching when I was twenty-two years old, only three years older than some of my students. Now, more than ever before, new teachers are entering our profession. I say good. New blood means new life! Combine this raw energy with the experience of the veterans and we stand a chance of accomplishing a thing or two. Watching as a young teacher finds his or her stride is invigorating; it recharges my batteries just like taking a class or putting together a book about this (a)vocation we call education.

May *The Quotable Teacher* bring the same amount of pleasure to you as it did to me. May it reflect the joy inherent in learning and in teaching.

Madison, CT
January 2003

The Quotable Teacher

1

The Importance of Teaching and Learning

The Miracle Worker, Anne Sullivan, once said that, "The highest result of education is tolerance." Would you expect anything less from a special education teacher? Tolerance is a lofty yet attainable goal; the rung that sits, I would imagine, just above love on Maslow's Hierarchy. At its best, tolerance is a knowledge of others that can lead to a greater knowledge of self. At its worst, a sympathetic smile.

The learning starts at home and continues as children grow out of the egocentric stage; as they become capable of not just acknowledging others but of helping them. Very little, though, can be tolerated without first being understood. This is where the teaching comes in.

The development of self-esteem is to the well-being of the individual as an understanding of diversity is to the well-being of a society. The person that cares for her or himself, just as s/he cares for others, is more than empathetic. S/he has learned acceptance. This is just one type of knowledge that we, as teachers, try to impart.

People also need wisdom and vocational skills to complement this altruism. Without math, we would live in huts instead of houses. Without science, we would not understand the weather or how to vaccinate. Without reading and writing, I would be telling stories to only those within earshot. And without social studies, we would be even more susceptible to the adage of history repeating itself. Without the arts, without physical education, without foreign languages . . .

Without teaching, there can be no learning. And without learning, there can be no advancement; not for individuals and not for society as a whole. Education is so important that this (almost) goes without saying.

I touch the future. I teach.

CHRISTA MCAULIFFE (1948–1986)

Life is an exciting business, and most exciting when it is lived for others.

HELEN KELLER (1880–1968)

Learning is not attained by chance, it must be sought for with ardor and attended to with diligence.

ABIGAIL ADAMS (1744–1818)

The one exclusive sign of thorough knowledge is the power of teaching.

ARISTOTLE (384–322 B.C.)

Blessed is the influence of one true, loving human soul on another.

GEORGE ELIOT (1819–1880)

Among the many purposes of schooling, four stand out to us as having special moral value: to love and care, to serve, to empower and, of course, to learn.

ANDY HARGREAVES AND MICHAEL FULLAN
What's Worth Fighting for Out There? (1998)

To me the sole hope of human salvation lies in teaching.

GEORGE BERNARD SHAW (1856–1950)

Any genuine teaching will result, if successful, in someone's knowing how to bring about a better condition of things than existed earlier.

JOHN DEWEY (1859–1952)

What office is there which involves more responsibility, which requires more qualifications, and which ought, therefore, to be more honorable, than that of teaching?

HARRIET MARTINEAU (1802–1876)

'Tis education forms the common mind
Just as the twig is bent, the tree's inclined.

ALEXANDER POPE
Moral Essays: Epistle to Richard Boyle, Earl of Burlington

Those who educate children are more to be honored than those who produce them; for these only gave them life, those the art of living well.

ARISTOTLE (384–322 B.C.)

Better than a thousand days of diligent study is one day with a great teacher.

JAPANESE PROVERB

There's no word in the language I revere more than "teacher." My heart sings when a kid refers to me as his teacher, and it always has. I've honored myself and the entire family of man by becoming a teacher.

PAT CONROY, *Prince of Tides* (1986)

Teaching is the world's most important job.

UNESCO (UNITED NATIONS EDUCATIONAL, SCIENTIFIC AND CULTURAL ORGANIZATION)

We cannot enter a learning society, an education age, without giving teachers the recognition they deserve.

FEDERICO MAYOR
DIRECTOR-GENERAL OF UNESCO, (1987–1999)

Teaching is a calling, not a choice.

MARY ANN ALEXANDER
COSMETOLOGY TEACHER IN YORKTOWN HEIGHTS, NEW YORK

———

Those who trust us educate us.

GEORGE ELIOT (1819–1880)

———

Education's purpose is to replace an empty mind with an open one.

MALCOLM S. FORBES (1919–1990)

A human being is not attaining his full heights until he is educated.

HORACE MANN (1796–1859)

He then learns that in going down into the secrets of his own mind he has descended into the secrets of all minds.

RALPH WALDO EMERSON (1803–1882)

Events in our classrooms today will prompt world events tomorrow.

J. LLOYD TRUMP (1908–)
AS QUOTED IN *The Teacher and the Taught* (1963)

Reading is to the mind, what exercise is to the body.

SIR RICHARD STEELE (1672–1729)

Education is a progressive discovery of our own ignorance.

WILL DURANT (1885–1981)

Whoso neglects learning in his youth, loses the past and is dead to the future.

EURIPIDES (480–406 B.C.)

Education is the point at which we decide whether we love the world enough to assume responsibility for it.

HANNAH ARENDT
Teaching as Leading

———

Aptitudes are assumed, they should become accomplishments. That is the purpose of all education.

JOHANN WOLFGANG VON GOETHE
Elective Affinities (1809)

———

Education is not a preparation for life; education is life itself.

JOHN DEWEY (1859–1952)

Education is not merely a means for earning a living or an instrument for the acquisition of wealth. It is an initiation into life of spirit, a training of the human soul in the pursuit of truth and the practice of virtue.

> VIJAYA LAKSHMI PANDIT (1900–1990)

What sculpture is to a block of marble, education is to a human soul.

> JOSEPH ADDISON (1672–1719)
> AS QUOTED IN *Spectator* (1711)

Education is the art of making man ethical.

> GEORG HEGEL
> *The Philosophy of Right* (1821)

Always to see the general in the particular is the very foundation of genius.

ARTHUR SCHOPENHAUER
Parerga and Paralipomena (1851)

———

Certain subjects yield a general power that may be applied in any direction and should be studied by all.

JOHN LOCKE (1632–1704)

———

In a completely rational society, the best of us would aspire to be teachers and the rest of us would have to settle for something less, because passing civilization along from one generation to the next ought to be the highest honor and highest responsibility anyone could have.

LEE IACOCCA
Iacocca (1986)

The principle goal of education is to create men who are capable of doing new things, not simply of repeating what other generations have done—men who are creative, inventive and discoverers.

JEAN PIAGET (1896–1980)

The elementary school must assume as its sublime and most solemn responsibility the task of teaching every child in it to read. Any school that does not accomplish this has failed.

WILLIAM J. BENNETT
"Report on Condition of Elementary Schools" (1986)

An educated man . . . is thoroughly inoculated against humbug, thinks for himself and tries to give his thoughts, in speech or on paper, some style.

ALAN SIMPSON ON BECOMING PRESIDENT OF VASSAR COLLEGE (1963)

Education is a specifically human activity. Unlike other animals, man inherits something over and above what is transmitted to him automatically by physical and psychic heredity.

ARNOLD J. TOYNBEE (1889–1975)
AS QUOTED IN *The Teacher and the Taught* (1963)

Education is the jewel casting brilliance into the future.

MARI EVANS (1923–)

Genius without education is like silver in the mine.

BENJAMIN FRANKLIN (1706–1790)

If you think education is expensive, try ignorance.

DEREK BOK
Universities and the Future of America (1990)

We can get over being poor, but it takes longer to get over being ignorant.

JANE SEQUICHIE HIFLER

Today our knowledge of the past is increasing at an unprecedented rate, and this at both ends of its ever lengthening vista. The archaeologists are making history by exhuming buried and forgotten civilizations as fast as the politicians are making it by taking new action for contemporary historians to study.

ARNOLD J. TOYNBEE (1889–1975)
AS QUOTED IN *The Teacher and the Taught* (1963)

Every man has a right to be wrong in his opinions, but no man has a right to be wrong in his facts.

BERNARD BARUCH
Baruch: My Own Story (1996)

We are born weak, we have need of help; we are born destitute of everything, we stand in need of assistance; we are born stupid, we have need of understanding. All that we are not possessed of at our birth, and which we require when we grow up, is bestowed on us by education.

JEAN JACQUES ROUSSEAU (1712–1778)

The whole object of education is . . . to develop the mind. The mind should be a thing that works.

SHERWOOD ANDERSON (1876–1941)

The utmost extent of man's knowledge is to know that he knows nothing.

JOSEPH ADDISON
Essay on Pride (1794)

The educated differ from the uneducated as much as the living from the dead.

ARISTOTLE (384–322 B.C.)

We live in a time of such rapid change and growth of knowledge that only he who is in a fundamental sense a scholar—that is, a person who continues to learn and inquire—can hope to keep pace, let alone play the role of guide.

NATHAN M. PUSEY
The Age of the Scholar (1963)

Our best chance for happiness is education.

MARK VAN DOREN (1894–1973)

Education is light, lack of it darkness.

RUSSIAN PROVERB

An age is called Dark not because the light fails to shine, but because people refuse to see it.

JAMES A. MICHENER (1907–1997)

Knowledge is the antidote to fear.

RALPH WALDO EMERSON (1803–1882)

Education is the mother and the father.

MOTTO OF THE "LOST BOYS OF THE SOUTHERN SUDAN," AS SEEN ON
60 Minutes (2001)

Not to know is bad;
not to wish to know is worse.

AFRICAN PROVERB

Seek knowledge from the cradle to the grave.

MUHAMMAD (571?–634?)

———

Wealth, if you use it, comes to an end; learning, if you use it, increases.

SWAHILI SAYING

———

If a man empties his purse into his head, no man can take it away from him. An investment in knowledge always pays the best interest.

BENJAMIN FRANKLIN (1706–1790)

The Great Society is a place where every child can find knowledge to enrich his mind and to enlarge his talents . . . It is a place where men are more concerned with the quality of their goals than the quantity of their goods.

LYNDON B. JOHNSON IN A SPEECH AT THE UNIVERSITY OF MICHIGAN
(1964)

The fortune of our lives therefore depends on employing well the short period of our youth.

THOMAS JEFFERSON IN A LETTER TO HIS DAUGHTER, MARTHA (1787)

Knowing is the measure of the man. By how much we know, so much we are.

RALPH WALDO EMERSON (1803–1882)

AS QUOTED IN *The Complete Works of Ralph Waldo Emerson*
(1893)

Life is indeed darkness save when there is urge,
And all urge is blind save when there is knowledge,
And all knowledge is vain save when there is work,
And all work is empty save when there is love.

KHALIL GIBRAN
The Prophet (1923)

If knowledge can create problems, it is not through ignorance that we can solve them.

ISAAC ASIMOV (1920–1992)

And what, Socrates, is the food of the soul? Surely, I said, knowledge is the food of the soul.

PLATO
Protagoras (380 B.C.)

By the worldly standards of public life, all scholars in their work are of course oddly virtuous.

JACOB BRONOWSKI IN A LECTURE AT THE MASSACHUSETTS INSTITUTE OF TECHNOLOGY (1953)

Unobstructed access to facts can produce unlimited good only if it is matched by the desire and ability to find out what they mean and where they lead.

NORMAN COUSINS
"Freedom as Teacher" (1981)

As our knowledge is converted to wisdom, the door to opportunity is unlocked.

BARBARA W. WINDER

I think, therefore I am.

RENÉ DESCARTES
Le Discours de la Méthode (1637)

What one doesn't understand one doesn't possess.

JOHANN WOLFGANG VON GOETHE
Art and Antiquity (1821)

The paradox of education is precisely this—that as one begins to become conscious one begins to examine the society in which he is being educated.

JAMES BALDWIN
"The Negro Child—His Self-Image" IN *The Saturday Review* (1963)

The very concept of history implies the scholar and the reader. Without a generation of civilized people to study history, to preserve its records, to absorb its lessons and relate them to its own problems, history, too, would lose its meaning.

George F. Kennan (1904–)

History not used is nothing, for all intellectual life is action, like practical life, and if you don't use the stuff—well, it might as well be dead.

Arnold J. Toynbee on *NBC* (1955)

A liberal education is at the heart of a civil society, and at the heart of a liberal education is the act of teaching.

A. Bartlett Giamatti
"The American Teacher" in *Harper's* (1980)

Let us think of education as the means of developing our greatest abilities, because in each of us there is a private hope and dream which, fulfilled, can be translated into benefit for everyone and greater strength for our nation.

JOHN F. KENNEDY (1917–1963)

2

The Backbone
of Democracy

As a teacher once told me, "Every great idea contains the seeds of its own heresy." Capitalism and democracy are two such ideas.

The United States was built on freedom and opportunity and, despite a history blemished by hypocrisy, continues to thrive as such. As a citizen and teacher of social studies, four pillars of this egalitarianism stand out to me: freedom of speech, the separation of church and state, the right to vote, and, of course, the right of every child living within our borders to a public education.

We are all aware of the plight of those schools that draw from an insufficient tax base. Anyone who has ever read Jonathan Kozol, scanned the newspaper for test scores, or bothered to research where dropout rates are highest knows that inequality reigns. Many of the writers quoted in the following pages predicted this unjust system long before the words "separate but equal" were first uttered. Capitalism, the engine that drives our democratic machine, is predicated on a fine understanding of human nature. Thinking that Americans could receive equal opportunity while being schooled under different circumstances reflects no understanding whatsoever.

Before my soapbox breaks, I would like to take a step back. First, we are to be congratulated for the effort we have made to desegregate. Bussing may be a terrible idea, but at least our hearts were in the right place. Second, we should be congratulated for attempting to educate *all* of our children. And finally, we should pat ourselves on the back for all of the individualized attention that is being given to children with special needs. Special education is no longer a converted broom closet in the basement.

I am still concerned about those students whose socioeconomic status inhibits their chances of ever going to college. They will not look into scholarships, let alone apply to schools, if they never graduate from high school. Too many of our young people are slipping away; there is no better vaccination against the American caste system than education. The underlying theme to life, liberty, and the pursuit of happiness, after all, is opportunity.

America is still the home to Horatio Algiers of all different backgrounds, but in the never-ending effort to improve the nation we cannot rest on our laurels. Our education system *should* be an example for all the world to follow. We can still be that city on a hill.

There is nothing wrong with America that cannot be cured by what is right with America.

WILLIAM JEFFERSON CLINTON (1946–)

Surely there is enough for everyone within this country. It is a tragedy that these good things are not more widely shared. All our children ought to be allowed a stake in the enormous richness of America.

JONATHAN KOZOL
Savage Inequalities: Children in America's Schools (1991)

If a free society cannot help the many who are poor, it cannot save the few who are rich.

JOHN F. KENNEDY IN HIS INAUGURAL ADDRESS (1961)

The education and empowerment of women throughout the world cannot fail to result in a more caring, tolerant, just and peaceful life for all.

AUNG SAN SUU KYI (1945–)

But the democratic promise of equal educational opportunity, half fulfilled, is worse than a promise broken. It is an ideal betrayed.

MORTIMER J. ADLER (1902–2001)
AS QUOTED IN *The Teacher and the Taught* (1963)

A little learning, indeed may be a dangerous thing, but the want of learning is a calamity to any people.

FREDERICK DOUGLASS (1817?–1895)

In West Germany . . . only 9 percent of the age cohort reached their terminal year of high school in the early 1970s, whereas in the U.S. approximately 75 percent did. It should not be surprising that a more academically select group would perform better than the average U.S. student.

CHESTER E. FINN, JR.
"The Drive for Educational Excellence" (1983)

Not until this century have we undertaken to give twelve years of schooling to all our children . . . Suffrage without schooling produces mobocracy, not democracy—not rule of law, not constitutional government by the people as well as for them.

MORTIMER J. ADLER
The Paideia Proposal: An Educational Manifesto (1982)

The important achievement of American education in the last thirty years in bringing a much larger proportion of our diverse society into the schools and succeeding with them there to some degree is not adequately recognized in the national debate about school quality. If we could get the youngsters who drop out of high school each year to stay there, it would cause another [test] score decline, and I'd be in favor of it.

HAROLD HOWE II
FROM HIS MARTIN BUSHKIN MEMORIAL LECTURE (1984)

If there is light in the soul
There will be beauty in the person.
If there is beauty in the person
There will be harmony in the house.
If there is harmony in the house
There will be order in the nation.
If there is order in the nation
There will be peace in the world.

CHINESE PROVERB

It takes all sorts to make a world.

ENGLISH PROVERB

Excellence is the best deterrent to racism or sexism.

OPRAH WINFREY (1954–)

The noblest aspect of the American liberal tradition is its respect for diversity.

THEODORE R. SIZER (1932–)

To refuse to face the task of creating a vision of a future America immeasurably more just and noble and beautiful than the America of today is to evade the most crucial, difficult, and important educational task.

GEORGE S. COUNTS (1889–1974)
AS QUOTED IN *The Teacher and the Taught* (1963)

It is incompatible with a democracy to train the many and educate the few.

ARTHUR BESTOR
AS QUOTED IN *The Great School Debate: Which Way for American Education* (1985)

I know no safe depository of the ultimate powers of the society but the people themselves; and if we think them not enlightened enough to exercise their control with a wholesome discretion, the remedy is not to take it from them but to inform their discretion.

THOMAS JEFFERSON (1743–1826)

Religious tolerance, mutual respect between vocational groups, belief in the rights of the individual are among the virtues that the best of our high schools now foster.

JAMES BRYANT CONANT (1893–1978)
AS QUOTED IN *The Teacher and the Taught* (1963)

I became a teacher because I wanted to help the underdog. Working with immigrants has made me more aware of my ancestors' plight when they came to America for a better life.

ELIZABETH BOWLER
ESOL TEACHER IN YORKTOWN HEIGHTS, NEW YORK (2001)

When I watch news footage of the day we entered school guarded by the 101st soldiers, I am moved by the enormity of that experience. I believe that was a moment when the whole nation took one giant step forward.

MELBA PATILLO BEALS ON THE INTEGRATION OF LITTLE ROCK
SCHOOLS
Warriors Don't Cry (1994)

What happens to a dream deferred? Does it dry up like a raisin in the sun?

LANGSTON HUGHES
"A Dream Deferred" (1926)

I believe in the existence of a great, immutable principle of natural law, or natural ethics which proves the absolute right of every human being that comes into the world to an education; and which, of course, proves the correlative duty of every government to see that the means of that education are provided for all.

HORACE MANN (1796–1859)

AS QUOTED IN *Places for Learning, Places for Joy: Speculations on American School Reform* BY THEODORE R. SIZER (1973)

Liberty cannot be preserved without general knowledge among the people.

JOHN ADAMS (1736–1826)

Few citizens really know what's going on in their schools. They settle for the familiar and ignore the substance.

THEODORE R. SIZER (1932–)

A society of free individuals in which all, through their own work, contribute to the liberation and enrichment of the lives of others, is the only environment in which any individual can really grow normally to his full stature.

JOHN DEWEY (1859–1952)

Freedom to think—which means nothing unless it means freedom to think differently—can be society's most precious gift to itself. The first duty of a school is to defend and cherish it.

ARTHUR BESTOR
AS QUOTED IN *The Teacher and the Taught* (1963)

What greater or better gift can we offer the republic than to teach and instruct our youth?

MARCUS T. CICERO (106–43 B.C.)

The main hope of a nation lies in the proper education of its youth.

DESIDERIUS ERASMUS (1466–1536)

Public education is the link between our nation and our dream of liberty and justice for all.

ELAINE GRIFFIN
1995 NATIONAL "TEACHER OF THE YEAR"

There is an old saying that the course of civilization is a race between catastrophe and education. In a democracy such as ours, we must make sure that education wins the race.

JOHN F. KENNEDY (1917–1963)

The most creative and emotionally engaged teachers see themselves not just as educating learners and workers, but as developing citizens.

ANDY HARGREAVES AND MICHAEL FULLAN
What's Worth Fighting for Out There? (1998)

All men by nature desire to know.

ARISTOTLE
Metaphysics (350 B.C.)

Information is the currency of democracy.

RALPH NADER (1934–)

The public schools, warts and all, was the single best thing about America. It was the only institution that said to one and all: "Come on! We don't care what color you are or what side of town you live on. Come on!" It was the closest we ever came to the American dream.

FROSTY TROY
"The Day the Schools Died" FROM THE *Oklahoma Observer* (1983)

If one accepts the ideal of a democratic, fluid society with a minimum of class distinction, the maximum of fluidity, the maximum of understanding between different vocational groups, then the ideal secondary school is a comprehensive public high school.

JAMES BRYANT CONANT (1893–1978)
AS QUOTED IN *The Teacher and the Taught* (1963)

A society that is concerned about the strength and wisdom of its culture pays careful attention to its adolescents.

THEODORE R. SIZER (1932–)

In an age when science is essential to our safety and to our economic welfare, it might be argued that a shortage of science teachers, and of scientists, is a clear and present danger to the nation.

> JAMES R. KILLIAN
> AS QUOTED in *The Teacher and the Taught* (1963)

But, because we dared to challenge the Southern tradition of segregation, this school became, instead, a furnace that consumed our youth and forged us into reluctant warriors.

> MELBA PATILLO BEALS ON THE INTEGRATION OF LITTLE ROCK SCHOOLS
> *Warriors Don't Cry* (1994)

All of us do not have equal talent, but all of us should have an equal opportunity to develop our talents.

JOHN F. KENNEDY (1917–1963)

Democratic communities help students to *be* as well as to *become*.

THOMAS J. SERGIOVANNI
Building Community in Schools (1994)

Upon the subject of education, I can only say that I view it as the most important subject which we as a people may be engaged in.

ABRAHAM LINCOLN (1809–1865)

Upon the education of the people of this country the fate of this country depends.

BENJAMIN DISRAELI (1804–1881)

I regret the trifling narrow contracted education of the females of my own country.

ABIGAIL ADAMS (1744–1818)

A good school is the price of peace in the community.

URSULA FRANKLIN IN HER OPENING ADDRESS AT THE CANADIAN EDUCATIONAL ASSOCIATION NATIONAL CONVENTION (1997)

We all, whether we know it or not, are fighting to make the kind of world that we should like.

OLIVER WENDELL HOLMES (1841–1935)
AS QUOTED IN *The Teacher and the Taught* (1963)

Education makes people easy to lead, but difficult to drive; easy to govern, but impossible to enslave.

HENRY PETER BROUGHAM IN A SPEECH TO THE HOUSE OF COMMONS (1828)

Jails and prisons are the complement of schools; so many less as you have of the latter, so many more must you have of the former.

HORACE MANN (1796–1859)

Every time you stop a school, you will have to build a jail.

MARK TWAIN IN A SPEECH (1900)

He who opens a school door, closes a prison.

VICTOR HUGO (1802–1885)

We must have a program to learn the way out of prison.

WARREN E. BURGER TO THE AMERICAN BAR ASSOCIATION (1981)

Only the educated are free.

EPICTETUS
Discourses (101 A.D.)

Learned Institutions ought to be favorite objects with
every free people. They throw that light over the public mind which is the best security against crafty and
dangerous encroachments on the public liberty.

JAMES MADISON (1751–1836)

Yet even as I wince at the terrible risk we all took, I remember thinking at the time that it was the right decision—because it felt as though the hand of fate was ushering us forward.

MELBA PATILLO BEALS ON THE INTEGRATION OF LITTLE ROCK SCHOOLS
Warriors Don't Cry (1994)

The benefits of education and of useful knowledge, generally diffused through a community, are essential to the preservation of a free government.

SAM HOUSTON (1793–1863)

In its education, the soul of a people mirrors itself.

LORD HALDANE
AS QUOTED IN *The Teacher and the Taught* (1963)

The essence of our effort to see that every child has a chance must be to assure each an equal opportunity, not to become equal, but to become different—to realize whatever unique potential of body, mind and spirit he or she possesses.

JOHN FISCHER
AS QUOTED IN THE *San Francisco Examiner* (1973)

As a product of the public education system, I want all American students to have what I had—access to a quality education that enables them to pursue any career they wish, and take on any challenge they choose. Giving our students the best education in the world is a moral imperative and, especially, an economic necessity.

RICHARD RILEY (1933–)

The ignorance of one voter in a democracy impairs the security of all.

JOHN F. KENNEDY AT VANDERBILT UNIVERSITY (1963)

A President must call on many persons—some to man the ramparts and to watch the far away, distant posts; others to lead us in science, medicine, education and social progress here at home.

LYNDON B. JOHNSON IN HIS ADDRESS TO THE WORLD EDUCATION CONFERENCE (1967)

Knowledge is the most democratic source of power.

ALVIN TOFFLER
Powershift: Knowledge, Wealth, and Violence at the Edge of the 21st Century (1990)

Oedipus tearing at his eyes, Lear in his demented eloquence upon the moors, Gloucester weeping from those "empty orbs"—these are the metaphors of cultural self-mutilation in a stumbling colossus. Eyeless at Gaza, Samson struggled to regain the power to pull down the pillars that destroyed him and his enemies together. The U.S. Bureau of the Census meanwhile sends out printed forms to ask illiterate Americans to indicate their reading levels.

JONATHAN KOZOL
Illiterate America (1985)

Which government is the best? The one that teaches us to govern ourselves.

JOHANN WOLFGANG VON GOETHE
Art and Antiquity (1826)

There are obvious places in which government can narrow the chasm between haves and have-nots. One is the public schools, which have been seen as the great leveler, the authentic melting pot.

ANNA QUINDLEN
AS QUOTED IN *The New York Times* (1992)

3

Those Who Teach

Thanksgiving is my favorite holiday. Family gathers for turkey and football while friends know just where to meet afterward. In light of September 11, there was even more reason to be thankful in 2001. That Sunday night, my mind raced: everything from the image of mourning families around incomplete tables to missing the people I'd just seen to getting back to work on *The Quotable Teacher*. So, I went online and asked friends and family to tell me about a favorite teacher. By 9:00 Monday morning I had an inbox full of e-mail.

One common response was knowledge of subject matter. Another was flexibility: it seems that many of the favorites were willing to accommodate individual learning styles. I enjoyed reading lengthy descriptions of creativity as well as tales of enthusiasm and it quickly became obvious that these memories would complement nicely the quotes I'd already collected. There were classroom antics and impassioned diatribes, feedback on written work (everything from red ink graffiti to smiley face stickers) and compliments that meant the world because of their scope and candor. It also helped to learn that our teachers were human beings just like us.

I knew that gathering personal accounts of great teaching would add depth to this chapter. What I didn't realize was how all of those e-mails would be such a strong reminder of who I want to be as a teacher.

———

Have you ever really had a teacher? One who saw you as a raw but precious thing, a jewel that, with wisdom, could be polished to a proud shine?

MITCH ALBOM
Tuesdays with Morrie (1997)

The best teachers I ever had were science teachers . . . thus my chosen profession! They were great because they loved their subject matter as much as I did and they inspired me to pursue my questions, curiosities, and interests. They were active, life-long learners and that rubbed off on me.

JIM GARDINEER
SCIENCE TEACHER IN MAHOPAC, NEW YORK (2002)

A good teacher is never done with their preparation—grading, evaluations, planning—because they are always trying to reinvent, improve, and inspire.

DR. DAVID CARLSON, DUKE UNIVERSITY '92 (2002)

Joe Rinaldi changed his teaching style to meet the student's learning needs. He never got frustrated when you didn't "get it." Instead, he changed the way he explained it.

DEBBIE SABATO
FOURTH GRADE TEACHER IN DENVER, COLORADO (2002)

I love to feel proud: proud of a child who learns the English language, proud of a child who makes the perfect M, proud of a child who acts like a friend and can be a model for the class, proud of a child who learns his or her line for the school play.

KAREN GUARDINO
KINDERGARTEN TEACHER IN SCARSDALE, NEW YORK (2002)

We make the road, others will make the journey.

VICTOR HUGO
"Thoughts" (TRANSLATED IN 1907)

Teaching gives me a greater sense of my own humanity.

CAMILLE BANKS-LEE
ENGLISH TEACHER IN OSSINING, NEW YORK (2002)

Parent indifference often rates above low teacher salaries as a cause of dissatisfaction for our nation's teachers.

MELITTA J. CUTRIGHT
The National PTA Talks to Parents: How to Get the Best Education for Your Child (1989)

The most admirable of reforms cannot but fall short in practice if teachers of sufficient quality are not available in sufficient quantity . . . Generally speaking, the more we try to improve our schools, the heavier the teacher's task becomes; and the better our teaching methods, the more difficult they are to apply.

JEAN PIAGET
Science of Education and the Psychology of the Child (1970)

Endeavor, first, to broaden your children's sympathies and, by satisfying their daily needs, to bring love and kindness into such unceasing contact with their impressions and their activity, that these sentiments may be engrafted in their hearts.

JOHANN HEINRICH PESTALOZZI (1746–1827)
AS QUOTED IN *The Teacher and the Taught* (1963)

Fifteen years after I sat on the big cozy rug in her kindergarten classroom, Ms. Cerbone remembered my name, the bows I used to wear in my hair, the dresses that my mom made for me. Each time we ran into each other, she would recall the memories with a smile. She never forgot.

KIM WALKLEY BUCKLEY, BEDFORD HILLS ELEMENTARY SCHOOL '81
(2002)

Teachers are more than any other class the guardians of civilization.

BERTRAND RUSSELL (1872–1970)
AS QUOTED IN *The Teacher and the Taught* (1963)

Each of Dr. Dominguez's classes were intense and draining, but worthwhile. He was the one teacher I could go to for advice and trust that I would get an honest answer.

SUZIE DEROBERTS, HARVARD UNIVERSITY '96 (2002)

Teachers teach because they care. Teaching young people is what they do best. It requires long hours, patience, and care.

HORACE MANN (1796–1859)

Time is the currency of teaching. We barter with time. Every day we make small concessions, small tradeoffs, but, in the end, we know it's going to defeat us.

ERNEST L. BOYER
"High School" (1983)

Behold, I do not give lectures or a little charity
When I give I give myself.

WALT WHITMAN (1819–1892)

Teaching is the best way I know of regaining balance
in your egocentric outlook on life.

BARBARA GASPARIK

CHILD DEVELOPMENT TEACHER IN YORKTOWN HEIGHTS, NEW
YORK (2002)

I still can not get used to how much my heart soars
with every student's success, and how a piece of my
heart is plucked away when any student slips away.

DELISSA L. MAI, NINTH GRADE TEACHER IN WYOMING

AS QUOTED IN *"What to Expect Your First Year of Teaching"*
(1998)

Unfortunately, teaching is often times like golf. So many bad shots in-between the good. And those are the few shots that we need to remember.

HOWARD NERO, FIFTH GRADE TEACHER IN NEW HAVEN, CONNECTICUT (2003)

There are a number of teachers I wouldn't mind buying a drink, but precious few I'd like to sit and talk with while they drink it.

GREG MACGILPIN, TEACHER'S COLLEGE COLUMBIA UNIVERSITY '00 (2003)

These children taught me a very simple but often overlooked principle. Believe in a child's power to succeed and they will succeed.

MAGGIE KEYSER
1999 DISNEY "TEACHER OF THE YEAR" FROM LAFAYETTE ELEMENTARY SCHOOL

Before I grew out of my shell, Ms. Sartor knew how shy I was. She wouldn't make me speak in front of the other students. Later, though, she would ask me questions, one-on-one.

WENDY JACKSON, WESTON ELEMENTARY SCHOOL '81 (2002)

Experienced teachers . . . are an invaluable resource to the [first-year] teachers who are willing to admit that they have much to learn.

ROBERT GRESS
TEACHER FROM LEXINGTON, KENTUCKY

Seek help. Always question us veteran teachers and we will find the answers together.

CAROL AVILA
TEACHER FROM RHODE ISLAND AND 1995 PRESIDENTIAL AWARD
WINNER FOR EXCELLENCE IN SCIENCE TEACHING

My first year has been as disappointing as it was rewarding . . . I have lost and found hope, reviewed and revised, and finally concluded that my presence here is much more important than I had thought it would be.

CATHERINE MCTAMANEY, HIGH SCHOOL TEACHER FROM TENNESSEE AS QUOTED IN *"What to Expect Your First Year of Teaching"* (1998)

None of my other teachers held me up to the same standard as my English teacher, Ms. Tsang. I eventually learned to hold myself up to the same standard.

MELISSA MACOMBER, THE BANCROFT SCHOOL '89 (2002)

The true teacher defends his pupils against his own personal influence.

AMOS BRONSON ALCOTT
"The Teacher" (1840)

I entered the classroom with the conviction that it was crucial for me and every other student to be an active participant, not a passive consumer . . . education that connects the will to know with the will to become.

BELL HOOKS
Teaching to Transgress (1994)

Good teaching is one-fourth preparation and three-fourths theatre.

GAIL GODWIN
The Odd Woman (1974)

Professor Rimmerman would bleed red ink all over your paper. You still might eke out a B, but he would definitely let you know what to work on next time around.

MARVIN T. LAO, HOBART COLLEGE '94 (2002)

Ms. Kenney taught me to love writing. Every story came back with a smiley face at the top of the page.

JOHN MCEDELMAN, BEDFORD VILLAGE ELEMENTARY SCHOOL '81 (2002)

I have been maturing as a teacher. New experiences bring new sensitivities and flexibility . . .

HOWARD LESTER
FIRST-YEAR TEACHER

I still felt the responsibility twenty-four hours a day! Teaching wasn't only my job, it was fast becoming my lifestyle.

SCOTT D. NIEMANN, THIRD AND FOURTH GRADE TEACHER IN ALASKA
AS QUOTED IN *"What to Expect Your First Year of Teaching"*
(1998)

Movie stars and rock musicians, athletes and models aren't heroes, they're celebrities. Heroes abound in public schools, a fact that doesn't make the news. There is no precedent for the level of violence, drugs, broken homes, child abuse, and crime in today's America. Public education didn't create these problems but deals with them every day.

FROSTY TROY
AS QUOTED IN THE *Oklahoma Observer* (2001)

In our world of big names, curiously, our true heroes tend to be anonymous. In this life of illusion and quasi-illusion, the person of solid virtues who can be admired for something more substantial than his well-knownness often proves to be the unsung hero: the teacher, the nurse, the mother, the honest cop, the hard worker at lonely, underpaid, unglamorous, unpublicized jobs.

DANIEL J. BOORSTIN
The Image (1961)

People snicker, "Those who can't do, teach." But, oh, how right they are. I could never, ever do all I dream of doing. I could never ever be an opera star, a baseball umpire . . . a great lover, a great liar, a trapeze artist, a writer, a dancer . . . or a thousand other aspirations I have had, while having only been given one thin ticket in this lottery of life!

ESMÉ RAJI CODELL
Educating Esmé (1999)

———

Teachers are the last bastion against darkness and ignorance. The intensity of this need was my surprise . . .

JAMES W. MORRIS, FIFTH GRADE TEACHER IN GEORGIA
AS QUOTED IN *"What to Expect Your First Year of Teaching"*
(1998)

A man should first direct himself in the way he should go. Only then should he instruct others.

BUDDHA (563–483 B.C.?)

———

He wanted everyone to know that he was at the school and of it, and that because of him and through the sheer force of his personality, the school was going to get better, improve, blaze into the heavens . . .

THOM JONES, *"Tarantula"* (2000)

Murray Cohn has, for twenty-three years, run Brandeis according to his own lights. He believes in cleanliness and order—and the halls of Brandeis are clean and orderly. He believes in homework, especially writing—and the students do it, even if they don't do enough. He believes in publicly praising achievement—and the school's bulletin boards offer congratulations to attendance leaders and the like. What Cohn and other administrators like him impart to their schools is nothing quantifiable; it is an ethos.

JAMES TRAUB
AS QUOTED IN *The Great School Debate: Which Way for American Education* (1985)

Compassionate teachers fill a void left by working parents who aren't able to devote enough attention to their children. A good education consists of much more than useful facts and marketable skills.

CHARLES PLATT

———•••———

It is the supreme art of the teacher to awaken joy in creative expression and knowledge.

ALBERT EINSTEIN

MOTTO FOR THE ASTRONOMY BUILDING AT PASADENA JUNIOR COLLEGE

———•••———

Who dares to teach, must never cease to learn.

JOHN COTTON DANA (1856–1929)

Rosie, an autistic child, talks to me now and can say her name. Possibly she could have reached these milestones in another classroom, but it happened in mine. What greater joy can a teacher feel than to witness a child's successes?

MICHELLE L. GRAHAM, FIRST GRADE TEACHER IN MINNESOTA
AS QUOTED IN *"What to Expect Your First Year of Teaching"*
(1998)

Ms. Tulin was funny, laid back, kind of funky. She allowed you to be a teenager but also demanded respect and order in the classroom. We learned about the Holocaust, survival in the wilderness, ourselves . . . and she was wonderful at facilitating all of this.

CARRIE PECK, FOX LANE MIDDLE SCHOOL '85 (2002)

Creativity does not exist on a continuum. Rather, there are small groups of teachers in every school that work in unique systems.

JIM SCHULZ
2000 DISNEY "TEACHER OF THE YEAR" FROM HELENA, MONTANA

It is written that he who governs well, leads the blind; but that he who teaches, gives them eyes.

DAVID O. MCKAY

The dream begins, most of the time, with a teacher who believes in you, who tugs and pushes and leads you on to the next plateau, sometimes poking you with a sharp stick called truth.

DAN RATHER (1931–)

A good professor is a bastard perverse enough to think what *he* thinks is important, not what government thinks is important.

EDWARD C. BANFIELD
AS QUOTED IN *Life* (1967)

You can't stop a teacher when they want to do something. They just *do* it.

J. D. SALINGER
The Catcher in the Rye (1951)

I don't think we expect enough of students. There are a lot of fabulous young people out there. They just need someone to show them the way.

RAFE ESQUITH, 1992 DISNEY "TEACHER OF THE YEAR" AND *Parent Magazine's* 1997 "TEACHER OF THE YEAR" FROM HOBART BOULEVARD ELEMENTARY SCHOOL IN LOS ANGELES, CALIFORNIA

Terry Culleton made *that* impact on me. "If you want a future in writing, I think you've got it," he wrote on one paper. "If you're willing to try."

KEITH DIXON, GEORGE SCHOOL '89 (2002)

————

I determined that there should not be a minute in the day when my children should not be aware of my face and my lips that my heart was theirs, that their happiness was my happiness, and their pleasures my pleasures.

JOHANN HEINRICH PESTALOZZI (1746–1827)
AS QUOTED IN *The Teacher and the Taught* (1963)

Most of us end up with no more than five or six people who remember us. Teachers have thousands of people who remember them for the rest of their lives.

ANDREW A. ROONEY (1919–)

I owe a lot to my teachers and mean to pay them back someday.

STEPHEN LEACOCK (1869–1944)

The good teacher makes the poor student good and the good student superior. When our students fail, we, as teachers, too, have failed.

MARVA COLLINS
Making a Difference in the Classroom (1992)

Mr. Shanley's kindness put me at ease and gave me confidence to learn. It's hard to absorb information when your brain is congested with doubt, and his encouragement helped me to relax and, in turn, to excel academically. He's the one I will remember because he's the one who seemed to care.

MEREDITH MCWADE, FOX LANE HIGH SCHOOL '89 (2002)

There are teachers of French and Spanish, Latin and Greek, who have worked for many years without ever seeing the countries whose spirits they have been endeavoring to evoke.

GILBERT HIGHET
The Immortal Profession (1976)

But the first day of school is our second New Year's. It is our day to make resolutions, to look backward to former lapses and triumphs and to look ahead, usually with a mix of anxiety and hope, to the year to come.

MARK EDMUNDSON
"Soul Training" IN *The New York Times Magazine* (2002)

Jade best describes the art of teaching because it is symbolic of growth. As a teacher you must always find new ways of growing, and you must always strive to find new ways of helping your students grow. Only in growth can the crop be harvested.

LYLEE STYLE
ENGLISH TEACHER IN YORKTOWN HEIGHTS, NEW YORK (2002)

Teachers long for respect and the autonomy that comes from it. They want the limits of their professional domain clearly outlined and their essential authority within it assured. They want physical, psychological, and economic protection.

THEODORE R. SIZER
Places for Learning, Places for Joy: Speculations on American School Reform (1973)

Good teaching is primarily an art, and can neither be defined or standardized ... Good teachers are born and made; neither part of the process can be omitted.

JOEL H. HILDEBRAND IN AN INTERVIEW CONDUCTED SHORTLY BEFORE HIS ONE HUNDREDTH BIRTHDAY

Teachers, I believe, are the most responsible and important members of society because their professional efforts affect the fate of the earth.

HELEN CALDICOTT (1938–)

He wished to teach, by example, that national boundaries and divisions between peoples ought not to exist: to show, even at the cost of his own career, that they are absurd.

GILBERT HIGHET ON ALBERT SCHWEITZER
The Immortal Profession (1976)

Choose a job you love, and you will never have to work a day in your life.

CONFUCIUS (C. 551–479 B.C.?)

Hope and its twin, possibility, best describe the art of teaching

CAMILLE BANKS-LEE
ENGLISH TEACHER IN OSSINING, NEW YORK (2002)

Good teachers are glad when a term begins and a little sad when it ends.

MARGARET MEAD (1901–1978)

Thirty-one chances. Thirty-one futures, our futures. It's an almost psychotic feeling, believing that part of their lives belongs to me. Everything they become, I also become. And everything about me, they helped to create.

ESMÉ RAJI CODELL
Educating Esmé (1999)

I was still learning when I taught my last class.

CLAUDE M. FUESS

I am quite sure that in the hereafter she will take me by the hand and lead me to my proper seat.

BERNARD BARUCH ON ONE OF HIS EARLY TEACHERS IN *News Summaries* (1955)

The fragrance always stays in the hand that gives the rose.

HADA BEJAR
Peacemaking Day by Day

The teaching goes on.

MITCH ALBOM
Tuesdays with Morrie (1999)

4

The Philosophy Behind Good Teaching

What was the compelling relationship in the movie *Ferris Bueller's Day Off*? You could argue that it was Ferris cajoling his passive sidekick, Cameron, into action. For my money, though, it was Principal Ed Rooney and his efforts to teach Ferris a lesson. Of course, in the end Ferris wins, Rooney loses, and we cheer. How can you argue with a day of truancy when it frees a young man from the paralyzing grip of his father? Throw in a parade and a day game at Wrigley Field and the question is mute. As Grace (Rooney's secretary) says of Ferris, "He's a righteous dude."

In *Welcome Back, Kotter* the righteous dude is the teacher, returned to his high school to help kids the same way that he was once helped. Mr. Kotter is so likable because in everything he does the students come first. His approach with the Sweathogs may seem to be nothing more than paternalistic, but there is real educational philosophy at work there. Nurturing his seeds to fruition, Mr. Kotter is happily, as Voltaire would say, tending his garden. Top-notch test scores are not a priority and assignments are a part of the curriculum only insofar as they promote dialogue between teacher and student. The real-life problems of the Sweathogs—and the subsequent teachable moments—are as important as anything Mr. Kotter ever gives for homework. There are episodes that touch upon suicide, alcoholism, fighting, boycotting cafeteria food, love, marriage, and divorce, and these leave Mr. Kotter no choice but to focus on the kids: he makes the conscious decision to shape lives and not just impart knowledge. And for this, guys like Vinny Barbarino, Horshack, Freddy "Boom Boom" Washington, and Epstein are forever grateful.

As you will see, some of history's finest minds (Aristotle and Plato, Roosevelt and Seneca, Thoreau and Dewey, Jung and Einstein) are in agreement with Mr. Kotter's values and methods. They might even go so far as to agree with Grace's assessment of Ferris.

At present there are differences of opinion . . . for all peoples do not agree as to the things that the young ought to learn, either with a view to virtue or with a view to the best life, nor is it clear whether their studies should be regulated more with regard to intellect or with regard to character.

ARISTOTLE (384–322 B.C.)

One looks back with appreciation to the brilliant teachers, but with gratitude to those who touched our human feelings.

CARL JUNG
Collected Works (1943)

Teaching is truth mediated by personality.

PHYLLIS BROOKS

I believe that education is a process of living and not a preparation for future living.

JOHN DEWEY
FROM A PAMPHLET PUBLISHED BY E. L. KELLOGG AND CO. (1897)

Teaching is an exhausting job. I did not, however, expect to be emotionally exhausted. I suppose the easiest way out of this dilemma would be to make myself emotionally unavailable to my students . . . Not this teacher. This teacher can't help but share in some of those emotional moments. I can't turn off a portion of myself when I walk into the classroom. It's either the whole Mrs. Baer or nothing.

ALLISON L. BAER, SIXTH GRADE TEACHER IN OHIO
AS QUOTED IN *"What to Expect in Your First Year of Teaching"* (1998)

We do not learn by inference and deduction and the application of mathematics to philosophy, but by direct intercourse and sympathy.

HENRY DAVID THOREAU
Natural History of Massachusetts (1842)

———

It has always seemed strange to me that in our endless discussions about education so little stress is laid on the pleasure of becoming an educated person, the enormous interest it adds to life. To be able to be caught up into the world of thought—that is to be educated.

EDITH HAMILTON (1867–1963)

To educate a man in mind and not in morals is to educate a menace to society.

THEODORE ROOSEVELT (1858–1919)

The aim of education is the knowledge, not of facts, but of values.

WILLIAM RALPH INGE (1860–1954)

An education that does not strive to promote the fullest and most thorough understanding of the world is not worthy of the name.

GEORGE S. COUNTS (1889–1974)
AS QUOTED IN *The Teacher and the Taught* (1963)

The important thing is not so much that every child should be taught, as that every child should be given the wish to learn.

JOHN LUBBOCK
The Pleasures of Life (1887)

Teachers should guide without dictating, and participate without dominating.

C. B. NEBLETTE

You cannot teach a man anything; you can only help him find it within himself.

GALILEO GALILEI (1564–1642)

Sometimes the last thing learners need is for their preferred learning style to be affirmed. Agreeing to let people learn only in a way that feels comfortable and familiar can restrict seriously their chance for development.

STEVEN BROOKFIELD

Keep on sowing your seed, for you never know which will grow—perhaps it all will.

ECCLESIASTES 11:6

I was always prepared for success but that means that I have to be prepared for failure, too.

SHEL SILVERSTEIN (1932–1999)
AS QUOTED IN *Publishers Weekly* (1974)

If history were taught in the form of stories, it would never be forgotten.

RUDYARD KIPLING (1865–1936)

Thought flows in terms of stories—stories about events, stories about people, and stories about intentions and achievements. The best teachers are the best storytellers. We learn in the form of stories.

FRANK SMITH

Tell me and I forget. Show me and I remember. Involve me and I understand.

CHINESE PROVERB

Setting an example is not the main means of influencing another, it is the only means.

ALBERT EINSTEIN (1879–1955)

———

Ms. Lambert gave us quizzes every day, not just as a way of dipsticking our understanding but as a means of evaluating her own clarity in teaching. I've never been so prepared for a class in my life.

SUZIE DEROBERTS, FOX LANE HIGH SCHOOL '92 (2002)

———

Teachers open the door, but you enter by yourself.

ANONYMOUS

The teacher who is indeed wise
Does not bid you to enter the house of his wisdom
But rather leads you to the threshold of your mind.

KHALIL GIBRAN
The Prophet (1923)

A great teacher never strives to explain his vision. He simply invites you to stand beside him and see for yourself.

R. INMAN

The mediocre teacher tells. The good teacher explains. The superior teacher demonstrates. The great teacher inspires.

WILLIAM ARTHUR WARD

The object of teaching a child is to enable him to get along without his teacher.

ELBERT HUBBARD (1856–1915)

If you can't explain it simply, you don't understand it well enough.

ALBERT EINSTEIN (1879–1955)

Teaching is the highest form of understanding.

ARISTOTLE (384–322 B.C.)

There is humane aggression in being a great teacher, as well as genuine love.

MARK EDMUNDSON
"Soul Training" IN *The New York Times Magazine* (2002)

The aim of education should be to teach us rather how to think, than what to think—rather to improve our minds, so as to enable us to think for ourselves, than to load the memory with the thoughts of other men.

JOHN DEWEY (1859–1952)
AS QUOTED IN *John Dewey on Education* (1964)

One of the least discussed ways of carrying a student through a hard unit of material is to challenge him with a chance to exercise his full powers, so that he may discover the pleasure of full and effective functioning . . .

JEROME S. BRUNER (1915–)
AS QUOTED IN *The Teacher and the Taught* (1963)

Direct the attention of your pupil to the phenomena of nature, and you will soon awaken his curiosity; but to keep that curiosity alive, you must be in no haste to satisfy it: he should not learn but invent the sciences.

JEAN JACQUES ROUSSEAU (1712–1778)

A master can tell you what he expects of you. A teacher, though, awakens your own expectations.

PATRICIA NEAL (1926–)

The art of teaching is the art of assisting discovery.

MARK VAN DOREN (1894–1973)

A sufficient experimental training was believed to have been provided as long as the student had been introduced to the results of past experiments or had been allowed to watch demonstration experiments conducted by his teacher, as though it were possible to sit in rows on a wharf and learn to swim merely by watching grown-up swimmers in the water.

JEAN PIAGET
Science of Education and the Psychology of the Child (1970)

There are some qualities which every teacher ought to possess—or train himself to possess. These are the qualities which he wants his pupils to acquire. The young learn much by the silent power of example.

GILBERT HIGHET
The Immortal Profession (1976)

The direction in which education starts a man will determine his future life.

PLATO (427?–347 B.C.)

The real difficulty, the difficulty which has baffled the sages of all times, is rather this: how can we make our teaching so potent in the emotional life of man, that its influence should withstand the pressure of the elemental psychic forces in the individual?

ALBERT EINSTEIN (1879–1955)

A teacher is one who makes himself progressively unnecessary.

THOMAS CARRUTHERS

An education isn't how much you have committed to memory, or even how much you know. It's being able to differentiate between what you do know and what you don't.

ANATOLE FRANCE (1844–1924)

To know how to suggest is the art of teaching.

HENRI FRÉDÉRIC AMIEL
Journal in Time (1864)

Acquire new knowledge whilst thinking over the old, and you may become a teacher of others.

CONFUCIUS (c. 551–479 B.C.?)

⸺•⸺

By viewing the old we learn the new.

CHINESE PROVERB

⸺•⸺

Knowledge can only be got in one way, the way of experience; there is no other way to know.

SWAMI VIVEKANANDA (1863–1902)

AS QUOTED IN *Living at the Source Yoga: Teachings of Vivekananda* (1993)

Enlighten the people generally, and tyranny and oppressions of body and mind will vanish like evil spirits at the dawn of day.

THOMAS JEFFERSON IN A LETTER TO DUPONT DE NEMOURS (1816)

What we learn with pleasure we never forget.

LOUIS MERCIER

To be conscious that we are perceiving and thinking is to be conscious of our own existence.

ARISTOTLE (384–322 B.C.)

We must beware of what I will call "inert ideas" that is to say, ideas that are merely received into the mind without being utilized or tested or thrown into fresh combinations.

ALFRED NORTH WHITEHEAD
Aims of Education and Other Essays (1967)

Education is not the piling on of learning, information, data, facts, skills, or abilities—that's training or instruction—but is rather a making visible what is hidden as a seed.

THOMAS MOORE (1779–1852)

In teaching, it is the method and not the content that is the message . . . the drawing out, not the pumping in.

ASHLEY MONTAGUE (1905–1999)

The teacher's task is not to implant facts but to place the subject to be learned in front of the learner and, through sympathy, emotion, imagination and patience, to awaken in the learner the restless drive for answers and insights which enlarge the personal life and give it meaning.

NATHAN M. PUSEY (1907–2001)
AS QUOTED IN *The New York Times* (1959)

The most important function of education at any level is to develop the personality of the individual and the significance of his life to himself and to others. This is the basic architecture of a life; the rest is ornamentation and decoration of the structure.

GRAYSON KIRK
AS QUOTED IN *Quote* (1963)

Education is a kind of continuing dialogue, and a dialogue assumes . . . different points of view.

ROBERT M. HUTCHINS ON ACADEMIC FREEDOM IN *Time* (1952)

Teaching is an instinctual art, mindful of potential, craving of realizations, a pausing, seamless process.

A. BARTLETT GIAMATTI
"The American Teacher" IN *Harper's* (1980)

A university's essential character is that of being a center of free inquiry and criticism—a thing not to be sacrificed for anything else.

RICHARD HOFSTADTER IN HIS COMMENCEMENT ADDRESS AT COLUMBIA UNIVERSITY (1968)

The ability to think straight, some knowledge of the past, some vision of the future, some skill to do useful service, some urge to fit that service into the well-being of the community—these are the most vital things education must try to produce.

VIRGINIA GILDERSLEEVE
Many a Good Crusade (1954)

The invention of IQ did a great disservice to creativity in education . . . Individuality, personality, originality, are too precious to be meddled with by amateur psychiatrists whose patterns for a "wholesome personality" are inevitably their own.

JOEL H. HILDEBRAND (1881–1983)
AS QUOTED IN *The New York Times* (1964)

. . . . philosophy lies deeper. It is not her office to teach men how to use their hands. The object of her lessons is to form the soul.

LUCIUS ANNAEUS SENECA
Epistulae ad Lucilium (63 A.D.)

———

To be a teacher in the right sense is to be a learner. I am not a teacher, only a fellow student.

SOREN KIERKEGAARD (1813–1855)

———

But this bridge will only take you halfway there—
The last few steps you'll have to take alone.

SHEL SILVERSTEIN
"This Bridge" FROM *A Light in the Attic* (1981)

5

The Need to Think Outside of the Box

The world was once as flat as a pancake. Or so we thought.

It is the willpower of individuals that buries the past and opens the door to the future. When he set sail, Christopher Columbus had a distinct purpose. He also had papal blessings and the latest nautical technology, the financial backing of a king and queen, and a crew made up, in part, of ex-convicts. There was tremendous risk, but the desire for wealth and truth outweighed that risk: a whole new world was waiting to be discovered. When he set sail, Christopher Columbus was being more than just creative, he was "thinking outside of the box."

When I first began teaching I heard this term quite often, but could only guess at its meaning. My administrator rarely modeled it and the examples my graduate school professor provided never applied to my students. The most important thing I learned during that first year was taught to me by those I was trying to teach: that different people experience the world in different ways and that these perspectives are not only healthy, they are a resource to be put to use. Unbeknownst to me, I had taken my first step toward thinking outside of the box.

A half-century after Columbus's arrival in the New World, Miguel de Cervantes created the first modern novel and literature's greatest idealist, sweetest romantic, and biggest dreamer. Readers still make the mistake of calling Don Quixote crazy when, in fact, he should be held up as an example of reality's pliability. We each see the world in our own way. Beauty is in the eye of the beholder.

Relating the author to the history of his native Spain, Carlos Fuentes described Cervantes as "caught between the flux of renewal and the stagnant waters of reaction." The same can be said of our schools. Educators are always looking to change the system, yet we remain mired in a factory-style environment of terminal points and quality control that smacks of political tunnel vision. We are working in the world of the Industrial Revolution even as we live in the world of the Technological Revolution. One aspect of teaching has not changed, though: a meaningful education requires a teacher who sees beauty where others see the ordinary.

We all know that the world is round. We are just now learning how small it can be. Television and the Internet have enhanced, for better and for worse, the background knowledge of students. This home base of information is vastly different from that of teachers, no matter how young those teachers might be. To adjust appropriately requires the initiative of Columbus and the vision of Quixote. And only a Rip Van Winkle (a parable of fear in the time of the Industrial Revolution) would be unaware of the impact that technology is having on learning. If our schools are to keep up, greater capital is required.

School districts are continually mining new resources; they must, otherwise teachers, and the tools of their trade, will be antiquated by the time freshmen become seniors. Thinking outside of the box now means signing partnerships with local businesses. It also means creating new opportunities for parental involvement and finding new and different ways to engage the students. We must all continue to think outside of the box.

Teachers have always been creative, just as the world has always been round. And like Don Quixote, teachers will continue to see Dulcinea's beauty . . . every time we take our place before a classroom full of students. It is a journey just like any other.

The greatest obstacle to discovering the shape of the earth, the continents, and the ocean was not ignorance but the illusion of knowledge.

DANIEL J. BOORSTIN
The Discoverers: A History of Man's Search to Know His World and Himself (1985)

The wrong way to teach history would be to show that there's only one perspective and only one history.

JONATHAN WENN
2001 DISNEY "TEACHER OF THE YEAR" FROM ROOSEVELT MIDDLE SCHOOL IN GLENDALE, NEW YORK

No one will live all his life in the world into which he was born, and no one will die in the world in which he worked in his maturity.

MARGARET MEAD (1901–1978)
AS QUOTED IN *The Teacher and the Taught* (1963)

Parents must acknowledge that the schooling, which will be best for their children in the twenty-first century, must be very different from the schooling they experienced themselves.

ANDY HARGREAVES AND MICHAEL FULLAN
What's Worth Fighting for Out There? (1998)

The same man cannot be skilled in everything, each has his own special excellence.

EURIPIDES (480–406 B.C.)

Acceptance of prevailing standards often means we have no standards of our own.

JEAN TOOMER (1894–1967)

———

As teachers, we must constantly try to improve schools and we must keep working at changing and experimenting and trying until we have developed ways of reaching every child.

ALBERT SHANKER (1928–1997)

Our school system has been constructed by conserva-
tives who were thinking much more in terms of fitting
our rising generations into the molds of traditional
learning than in the terms of training inventive and critical minds. From the point of view of society's present
needs, it is apparent that those old molds are cracking ...

JEAN PIAGET
Science of Education and the Psychology of the Child (1970)

It is our American habit if we find the foundations of
our educational structure unsatisfactory to add another story or wing. We find it easier to add a new study
or course or kind of school than to recognize existing
conditions so as to meet the need.

JOHN DEWEY (1859–1952)

School buildings mirror our educational concepts. America has a predilection for straight lines, rectangles, squared-off blocks, and nowhere is this more true than in the usual schoolhouse.

J. LLOYD TRUMP (1908–)
AS QUOTED IN *The Teacher and the Taught* (1963)

All genuine learning is active, not passive. It involves the use of the mind, not just the memory. It is a process of discovery, in which the student is the main agent, not the teacher.

MORTIMER J. ADLER
The Paideia Proposal: An Educational Manifesto (1982)

One of the great strengths of caring as an ethic is that it does not assume that all students should be treated by some impartial standard of fairness. Some students need more attention than others . . .

NEL NODDINGS
Caring: A Feminist Perspective (1984)

Since there is no single set of abilities running throughout human nature, there is no single curriculum which all should undergo. Rather, the schools should teach everything that anyone is interested in learning.

JOHN DEWEY (1859–1952)

Mr. Ehrhard was so interesting that you absolutely wanted to share in everything he cared about. He was the physics teacher who recommended *The Catcher in the Rye* and we all read it, of our own free will.

ALICIA SOLÍS, WESTON HIGH SCHOOL '90 (2002)

We have to look for routes of power our teachers never imagined, or were encouraged to avoid.

THOMAS PYNCHON
Gravity's Rainbow (1973)

There is a new science of complexity which says that the link between cause and effect is increasingly difficult to trace; that change (planned or otherwise) unfolds in non-linear ways; that paradoxes and contradictions abound; and that creative solutions arise out of diversity, uncertainty and chaos.

ANDY HARGREAVES AND MICHAEL FULLAN
What's Worth Fighting for Out There? (1998)

———

At a time when we should be opening doors to the future, we are fossilizing a curriculum and a kind of teaching that seemed to make sense in the 1950s.

THOMAS SOBOL IN HIS CLOSING ADDRESS TO THE SUMMER LAW
INSTITUTE AT COLUMBIA UNIVERSITY (2000)

We are being sold a bill of goods when it comes to talking about tougher standards for our schools. The standards movement is pushing teachers and students to focus on memorizing information, then regurgitating fact for high test scores. The shift is away from teaching students to be thinkers who can make sense of what they're learning.

ALFIE KOHN
The Case Against Standardized Testing (2000)

Ideas, facts, relationships, stories, histories, possibilities, artistry in words, in sounds, in form and in color, crowd into the child's life, stir his feelings, excite his appreciation, and incite his impulses to kindred activities. It is a saddening thought that on this golden age there falls so often the shadow of the crammer.

ALFRED NORTH WHITEHEAD (1861–1957)
AS QUOTED IN *The Teacher and the Taught* (1963)

Recognizing a correct answer out of a predetermined list of responses is fundamentally different from the act of reading, or writing, or speaking, or reasoning, or dancing, or anything else that human beings do in the real world.

LINDA DARLING-HAMMOND
"Mad-Hatter Tests of Good Teaching" IN The New York Times (1984)

Teaching consists of causing people to go into situations from which they cannot escape, except by thinking. Do not handicap your children by making their lives easy.

ROBERT HEINLEIN
The Notebooks of Lazarus Long (1973)

You need to have a plan of sorts but don't become consumed by it. Winds change . . .

JOSEPH EHRHARD
PHYSICS TEACHER FROM WESTON, CONNECTICUT (1990)

It is in fact nothing short of a miracle that the modern methods of instruction have not yet entirely strangled the holy curious of inquiry.

ALBERT EINSTEIN (1879–1955)

Restlessness and discontent are the first necessities of progress.

THOMAS A. EDISON (1847–1931)

Teachers who really value their emotional bonds to students are willing to experiment with alternative structures that make these bonds stronger.

ANDY HARGREAVES AND MICHAEL FULLAN
What's Worth Fighting for Out There? (1998)

There are many who lust for the simple answers of doctrine or decree. They are on the left and right. They are not confined to a single part of the society. They are terrorists of the mind.

A. BARTLETT GIAMATTI IN HIS FINAL BACCALAUREATE ADDRESS (1986)

The great secret of education is to make the exercises of the body and the mind serve as a relaxation to each other.

JEAN JACQUES ROUSSEAU (1712–1778)

The real crisis of education is the crisis of a society that in the race for renewed hegemony in the world trading order . . . is concerned most with technical proficiency among its graduates—ensuring workers who will know more and more about less and less in regard to the world they inhabit and the work they do.

SVI SHAPIRO
"Education Crisis or Social Crisis" (1983)

It is not in the power of one generation to form a complete plan of education.

IMMANUEL KANT (1724–1804)
AS QUOTED IN *The Teacher and the Taught* (1963)

[It was] an initiation into the love of learning, of learning how to learn, that was revealed to me by my BLS masters as a matter of interdisciplinary cognition—that is, learning to know something by its relation to something else.

LEONARD BERNSTEIN ON BOSTON LATIN SCHOOL
AS QUOTED IN *The New York Times* (1984)

Universities should be safe havens where ruthless examination of realities will not be distorted by the aim to please or inhibited by the risk of displeasure.

KINGMAN BREWSTER IN HIS INAUGURAL ADDRESS AT YALE UNIVERSITY (1964)

No matter how deep a study you make, what you really have to rely on is your own intuition and when it comes down to it, you really don't know what's going to happen until you do it.

KONOSUKE MATSUSHITA (1894–1989)
AS QUOTED IN *Matsushita Leadership* (1997)

Conformity is the jailer of freedom and the enemy of growth.

JOHN F. KENNEDY IN HIS ADDRESS TO THE UNITED NATIONS GENERAL ASSEMBLY (1961)

A little knowledge that acts is worth infinitely more than much knowledge that is idle.

KHALIL GIBRAN (1883–1931)
AS QUOTED IN *A Second Treasury of Khalil Gibran* (1962)

American history is longer, larger, more various, more beautiful, and more terrible than anything anyone has ever said about it.

JAMES BALDWIN
"A Talk to Teachers" (1963)

Has there ever been a society which has died of dissent? Several have died of conformity in our lifetime.

JACOB BRONOWSKI IN A LECTURE AT MASSACHUSETTS INSTITUTE OF TECHNOLOGY (1953)

What a glorious gift is imagination, and what satisfaction it affords!

THOMAS MANN
Confessions of Felix Krull, Confidence Man (1954)

———

Talent is like electricity. We don't understand electricity. We use it.

MAYA ANGELOU (1928–)
AS QUOTED IN *Black Women Writers at Work* (1983)

I was able to find nontraditional methods in the traditional setting of business school. All of us were subject to three "cold calls" and our performance would determine one-third of our grade. Bill could nail us at any time, in class or in the hallway, at a bar or at the apartment, and you had to answer. Incidentally, as tough as his course was, it was the most oversubscribed in the school.

JOHN KELLY ON BILL COCKRUM, FINANCE PROFESSOR AT ANDERSON
BUSINESS SCHOOL AND INNOVATOR OF THE COLD CALL METHOD OF
ASSESSMENT (2002)

The most extraordinary thing about a really good teacher is that he or she transcends accepted educational methods.

MARGARET MEAD (1901–1978)
AS QUOTED IN *The Teacher and the Taught* (1963)

Education in this country has steadily improved since the systematic study of the science of education was started about 1890. No doubt it will continue to improve at about the same speed, and schools in the year 2000 will be somewhat better than they are today. The question is, could they be better than that?

J. LLOYD TRUMP (1908–)
AS QUOTED IN *The Teacher and the Taught* (1963)

6

That's What
the Silence Is For:
The Process of Learning

Educators are constantly evaluating how we can have the greatest impact on students. In addition to our style of instruction, we must look closely at the materials we use and the work that we assign. In this era of high stakes testing, curriculum decisions are more important than ever; hours are spent discussing curriculum on the department, grade, school, and district levels. At the heart of these discussions is the process of learning.

As teachers, we must constantly educate ourselves not only about available materials but also about theories of learning. Although these theories can be applied to the whole class, I like to utilize them in a more individualistic manner. Here is one example: Harvard professor of psychology Howard Gardner, well-known for his theory of multiple intelligences, asserts that every student excels in at least one area (of "intelligence") and that it behooves the teacher to maximize on this strength. A young ballerina, for example, may benefit in more ways than one from her knowledge of body and movement. Her love of dance—a love that is most likely the result of her ability *to* dance—may enable her to learn about foreign cities, their history and their language, as she investigates the world's finest ballet companies. To go a step further, the teacher who subscribes to Gardner's theory will be aware of this interest and somehow incorporate ballet into assignments and projects.

Not all questions can be answered with Howard Gardner, though. I recently learned of the permanent damage done to children who cannot read by the end of third grade. Dr. Jerry Graniero, in discussing the importance of trying different methods of instruction, stated that, "By the age of ten the brain may actually start to destroy unused synapses." Essentially, a child who is not given the opportunity, on a daily basis, to use different parts of the brain is being put in harm's way. The teacher must arrange a variety of activities.

A few weeks later, I was taught something else about how people learn. The school's speech therapist and I were working with a third grade girl who has cerebral palsy. This is a child who has a positive attitude, a great memory, and works hard; unfortunately, it is unlikely that she will ever be able to talk. The speech therapist told me to *wait*, rather than prompt her to communicate with us (she uses PECS picture cards). "Oftentimes, the learning happens in these uncomfortable moments. That's what the silence is for." Never would I have thought that I could best help a student by *not* helping her.

Curriculum decisions require much research and discussion. In taking the time to determine the best way to deliver instruction, educators can really have an impact on student learning. The answer does not always come with a committee deciding to reallocate the budget or with an administrator unearthing the latest and greatest staff development. Sometimes the answer comes with wisdom shared between colleagues. When a teacher is having trouble, the hope is that another teacher will be able to offer up a few leads. Sharing an article about Gardner's multiple intelligences might reveal the answer. Or perhaps the opposite is more appropriate: a project that requires kids to be visual, auditory, *and* tactile learners. The solution could be even simpler than that. I am just now learning that it might be as easy as waiting it out.

The educator must above all understand how to wait; to reckon all effects in the light of the future, not of the present.

ELLEN KEY (1849–1926)

I believe that children learn best when given the opportunity to taste, feel, see, hear, manipulate, discover, sing, and dance their way through learning.

KATY GOLDMAN, TEACHER FROM PINE, ARIZONA
AS QUOTED IN *"Survival Guide for New Teachers"* (2002)

———

I cannot teach anybody anything, I can only make them think.

SOCRATES (469–399 B.C.)

———

Only the curious will learn and only the resolute overcome the obstacles to learning. The quest quotient has always excited me more than the intelligence quotient.

EUGENE S. WILSON
AS QUOTED IN THE *Reader's Digest* (1968)

I was taught that the way of progress is neither swift nor easy.

MARIE CURIE (1867–1934)

One can think effectively only when one is willing to endure suspense and to undergo the trouble of searching.

JOHN DEWEY (1859–1952)

It's not that I'm so smart, it's just that I stay with problems longer.

ALBERT EINSTEIN (1879–1955)

Men learn while they teach.

> LUCIUS ANNAEUS SENECA
> *Ad Lucilium Epistulae Morales*

The essence of learning is the ability to manage change by changing yourself.

> A. DE GUES
> *The Living Company* (1997)

He is educated who knows where to find out what he doesn't know.

> GEORG SIMMEL (1858–1918)

Too often, for too many of us, learning appears to be an imposition, a surrender of our own will power to external direction, indeed a sort of enslavement.

GILBERT HIGHET
The Immortal Profession (1976)

Even without success, creative persons find joy in a job well done. Learning for its own sake is rewarding.

MIHALY CSIKSZENTMIHALYI
Creativity: Flow and the Psychology of Discovery and Invention (1997)

The wisest mind has something yet to learn.

GEORGE SANTAYANA (1863–1952)

The illiterate of the twenty-first century will not be those who cannot read and write, but those who cannot learn, unlearn, and relearn.

ALVIN TOFFLER
Powershift: Knowledge, Wealth, and Violence at the Edge of the 21st Century (1990)

How sustained an episode a learner is willing to undergo depends upon what the person expects to get from his efforts, in the sense of such external things as grades but also in the sense of a gain in understanding.

JEROME S. BRUNER (1915–)
AS QUOTED IN *The Teacher and the Taught* (1963)

Learning is a social process that occurs through inter-personal interaction within a cooperative context. Individuals, working together, construct shared under-standings and knowledge.

DAVID JOHNSON
Active Learning: Cooperation in the College Classroom (1991)

Learning by discovery can occur without help, but only geniuses can educate themselves without the help of teachers.

MORTIMER J. ADLER
The Paideia Proposal: An Educational Manifesto (1982)

The shrewd guess, the fertile hypothesis, the courageous leap to a tentative conclusion—these are the most valuable coins of the thinker at work. But in most schools guessing is heavily penalized and is associated somehow with laziness.

JEROME S. BRUNER
The Process of Education (1960)

Learning is often spoken of as if we were watching the open pages of all the books which we have ever read, and then, when occasion arises, we select the right page to read aloud to the universe.

ALFRED NORTH WHITEHEAD (1861–1957)
AS QUOTED IN *The Teacher and the Taught* (1963)

Where I grew up, learning was a collective activity. But when I got to school and tried to share learning with other students that was called cheating. The curriculum sent the clear message to me that learning was a highly individualistic, almost secretive, endeavor.

HENRY A. GIROUX
Border Crossings (1992)

Try to put into practice what you already know, and in so doing you will in good time discover the hidden things which you now inquire about.

HENRY VAN DYKE (1852–1933)

Our errors are surely not such awfully solemn things. In a world where we are so certain to incur them in spite of all our caution, a certain lightness of heart seems healthier than this excessive nervousness on their behalf.

> WILLIAM JAMES
> *"The Will to Believe"* (1897)

Mistakes are the portals of discovery.

> JAMES JOYCE
> *Dubliners* (1914)

I have learned throughout my life as a composer chiefly through my mistakes and pursuits of false assumptions, not my exposure to founts of wisdom and knowledge.

> IGOR STRAVINSKY (1882–1971)

Every act of conscious learning requires the willingness to suffer an injury to one's self-esteem. That is why young children, before they are aware of their own self-importance learn so easily; and why older persons, especially if vain or important, cannot learn at all.

THOMAS SZASZ
The Second Sin (1973)

If a man will begin with certainties, he shall end in doubts; but if he will be content to begin with doubts, he shall end in certainties.

FRANCIS BACON
The Advancement of Learning (1605)

To every answer you can find a new question.

YIDDISH PROVERB

It is what we think we know already that often prevents us from learning.

CLAUDE BERNARD (1813–1878)

I find that a great part of the information I have was acquired by looking up something and finding something else on the way.

FRANKLIN P. ADAMS (1881–1960)

In completing one discovery we never fail to get an imperfect knowledge of others of which we could have no idea before, so that we cannot solve one doubt without creating several new ones.

JOSEPH PRIESTLY (1733–1804)

They know enough who know how to learn.

HENRY B. ADAMS (1838–1918)

———

For many, learning is a spiral, where important themes are visited again and again throughout life, each time at a deeper, more penetrating level.

JEROLD W. APS
Teaching from the Heart (1996)

———

In all things we learn only from those we love.

JOHANN WOLFGANG VON GOETHE (1749–1832)

One must learn by doing the thing, for though you think you know it, you have no certainty until you try.

ARISTOTLE (384–322 B.C.)

Much that passes for education . . . is not education at all but ritual. The fact is that we are being educated when we know it least.

DAVID P. GARDNER
Vital Speeches (1975)

A teacher who is attempting to teach without inspiring the pupil with a desire to learn is hammering on a cold iron.

HORACE MANN (1796–1859)

Anxiety checks learning. An overall feeling of inferiority, a temporary humiliation, a fit of depression, defiance or anger, a sense of being rejected, and many other emotional disturbances affect the learning process. The reverse is true; a feeling of well-being and of being respected by others stimulates an alert mind, willingness to participate, and an attitude conducive to learning.

EDA LESHAN
The Conspiracy against Childhood (1967)

The result of the educative process is capacity for further education.

JOHN DEWEY (1859–1952)

In its broadest sense, learning can be defined as a process of progressive change from ignorance to knowledge, from inability to competence, and from indifference to understanding.

CAMERON FINCHER
"Learning Theory and Research" (1994)

My advice to kids who want to become authors and to kids who just want to write well just for fun is to read. I think that we really learn how to write by reading.

JOANNA COLE (1944–)
AUTHOR OF *The Magic School Bus* SERIES

Reading well makes children more interesting both to themselves and others, a process in which they will develop a sense of being separate and distinct selves.

HAROLD BLOOM

Short Stories and Poems for Exceptionally Intelligent Children (2001)

———

Where there is an open mind there will always be a frontier.

CHARLES F. KETTERING (1876–1958)

———

Education is man's going forward from cocksure ignorance to thoughtful uncertainty.

KENNETH G. JOHNSON

Learning proceeds in fits and starts.

JEROLD W. APS
Teaching from the Heart (1996)

———•••———

Most people would say that what I am doing is "learning to play" the cello. But these words carry into our minds the strange idea that there exists two very different processes: 1) learning to play the cello; and 2) playing the cello . . . We learn to do something by doing it. There is no other way.

JOHN HOLT (1923–1985)

Education is a lifelong process of which schooling is only a small but necessary part. As long as one remains alive and healthy, learning can go on—and should.

MORTIMER J. ADLER
The Paideia Proposal: An Educational Manifesto (1982)

True interest appears when the self identifies itself with ideas or objects, when it finds in them a means of expression and they become a necessary form of fuel for its activity.

JEAN PIAGET
Science of Education and the Psychology of the Child (1970)

Most of the most important experiences that truly educate cannot be arranged ahead of time with any precision.

HAROLD TAYLOR

AS QUOTED IN *The Saturday Review* (1961)

The very fact of its finding itself in agreement with other minds perturbs it, so that it hunts for points of divergence, feeling the urgent need to make it clear that at least it reached the same conclusions by a different route.

SIR HERBERT BUTTERFIELD IN HIS RETIREMENT ADDRESS (1961)

We learn simply by the exposure of living, and what we learn most natively is the tradition in which we live.

DAVID P. GARDNER
Vital Speeches (1975)

Learning is like rowing upstream. Advance or lose all.

ANONYMOUS

Learning is always rebellion ... Every bit of new truth discovered is revolutionary to what was believed before.

MARGARET LEE RUNBECK

Learning without thought is labor lost.

CONFUCIUS (c. 551–479 B.C.?)

It is by extending oneself, by exercising some capacity previously unused that you come to a better knowledge of your own potential.

HAROLD BLOOM
Short Stories and Poems for Exceptionally Intelligent Children (2001)

That is the essence of science: ask an impertinent question, and you are on the way to a pertinent answer.

JACOB BRONOWSKI
The Ascent of Man (1973)

———•◦•———

That's what learning is, after all; not whether we lose the game, but how we lose and how we've changed because of it and what we take away from it that we never had before . . .

RICHARD BACH
The Bridge Across Forever (1984)

Art is not to be taught in Academies. It is what one looks at, not what one listens to, that makes the artist. The real schools should be the streets.

OSCAR WILDE
"The Relation of Dress to Art" IN THE *Pall Mall Gazette* (1885)

I am still learning.

MICHELANGELO BUONARROTI (1475–1564)

7

Discipline and Classroom Management

The first time I ever had students to call my own, I didn't have to worry about discipline. This is because my students came to class with their prison guards.

Actually, they were called "cadres" and they were National Guardsmen involved in ChalleNGe, a program for at-risk kids. While I taught, these cadres kept a close eye on the "cadets." If one of them misbehaved, a cadre simply yelled, "Drop and give me twenty!" And the offender obliged.

Short-term, this was great: I experienced educational bliss, the ability to teach without an ounce of concern for behavior. Long-term, this situation was also beneficial: I saw how I never again wanted my classroom to be.

I was a teacher in their program, so I had to comply with their rules—no matter how severe. Today, when I think of discipline I do not think of push-ups just as when I think of students I do not think of soldiers. I work under the assumption that if a class is well-managed, if students are continually engaged in a meaningful manner and treated as the important individuals that they are, then in most cases minimal behavior problems will occur. A majority of the quotes I've chosen reflect this belief.

———

Patience is the key to paradise.

ARMENIAN PROVERB

———

The more you prepare outside class, the less you
    perspire in class.
The less you perspire in class, the more you inspire
    the class.

HO BOON TIONG
"PRACTISING REFLECTIVE TEACHING" (2001)

The secret of education is respecting the pupil.

RALPH WALDO EMERSON (1803–1882)

———

Have a heart that never hardens, and a temper that never fires, and a touch that never hurts.

CHARLES DICKENS (1812–1870)

———

You cannot shake hands with a clenched fist.

INDIRA GANDHI (1917–1984)
AS QUOTED IN THE *Christian Science Monitor* (1982)

The key to everything is patience. You get the chicken by hatching the egg—not by smashing it.

ELLEN GLASGOW (1873–1945)

The shell must be cracked apart if what is in it is to come out, for if you want the kernel you must break the shell.

MEISTER ECKHART

He who wrestles with us strengthens our nerves and sharpens our skills.

EDWARD BURKE

Education is the ability to listen to almost anything without losing your temper or your self-confidence.

ROBERT FROST (1874–1963)

Do not train a child to learn by force or harshness; but direct them to it by what amuses their minds, so that you may be better able to discover with accuracy the peculiar bent of the genius of each.

PLATO (427?–347 B.C.)

The powers of students sometimes sink under too great severity in correction . . . while they fear everything, they cease to attempt anything.

QUINTILIAN (c. 35–95 A.D.)
AS QUOTED IN *The Teacher and the Taught* (1963)

Love them enough to risk their not liking you. Children must know that there are consequences to be suffered when they are not nice.

CAROL AVILA

TEACHER FROM RHODE ISLAND AND 1995 PRESIDENTIAL AWARD WINNER FOR EXCELLENCE IN SCIENCE TEACHING

A wise man knows and will keep his place; but a child is ignorant of his, and therefore cannot confine himself to it. There are a thousand avenues through which he will be apt to escape; it belongs to those who have the care of his education, therefore, to prevent him; a task, by the way, which is not very easy.

JEAN JACQUES ROUSSEAU (1712–1778)

AS QUOTED IN *The Teacher and the Taught* (1963)

Fun is a good thing but only when it spoils nothing better.

GEORGE SANTAYANA
The Sense of Beauty (1896)

The wise adapt themselves to circumstances, as water molds itself to the pitcher.

CHINESE PROVERB

Children who are forced to eat acquire a loathing for food, and children who are forced to learn acquire a loathing for knowledge.

BERTRAND RUSSELL (1872–1970)
AS QUOTED IN *The Teacher and the Taught* (1963)

Describing her first day back in grade school, after a long absence, a teacher said, "It was like trying to hold thirty-five corks under water at the same time."

MARK TWAIN (1835–1910)

School disruption comes from those children who have given up hope of trying to learn anything.

ALBERT SHANKER
"Discipline: The Political Football" (1984)

All genuine education is liberating, and certainly needs freedom and discipline.

REGINALD D. ARCHAMBAULT
John Dewey on Education (1964)

The teachers who get "burned out" are not the ones who are constantly learning, which can be exhilarating, but those who feel they must stay in control and ahead of the students at all times.

FRANK SMITH

If I compliment them, I mean it. If I don't think they are doing a good job, I lay it on the line. I demand respect from them and I give them respect, and I think they are important.

LENNI ABEL
ART TEACHER AND 2000 DISNEY "TEACHER OF THE YEAR" FROM THE BRONX

I let the kids know exactly what I expect. I praise them when they meet those expectations and point it out to them when they don't.

RON CLARK
FIFTH GRADE TEACHER AND 2000 DISNEY "TEACHER OF THE YEAR" FROM HARLEM

There are two sides to every story and TRUTH lays somewhere in the middle.

JEAN GATI

Let the *no!* once pronounced, be as a brazen wall, against which when a child hath some few times exhausted his strength without making any impression, he will never attempt to overthrow it again.

JEAN JACQUES ROUSSEAU (1712–1778)
AS QUOTED IN *The Teacher and the Taught* (1963)

No use to shout at them to pay attention. If the situations, the materials, the problems before the child do not interest him, his attention will slip off to what does interest him, and no amount of exhortation of threats will bring it back.

JOHN HOLT (1923–1985)

However much the teacher is tempted to treat the exceptional pupil (whether very good or very bad) as a special case and to devote to him or her a great deal of time and attention, he must remember that this is not his sole duty, and usually is not his main duty. His first obligation is to his class: to the group.

GILBERT HIGHET
The Immortal Profession (1976)

People's behavior makes sense if you think about it in terms of their goals, needs, and motives.

THOMAS MANN (1875–1955)

———•◆•———

Many instructional arrangements seem "contrived," but there is nothing wrong with that. It is the teacher's function to contrive conditions under which students learn. It has always been the task of formal education to set up behavior which would prove useful or enjoyable later in a student's life.

B. F. SKINNER
Science and Human Behavior (1953)

If a doctor, lawyer, or dentist had forty people in his office at one time, all of whom had different needs, and some of whom didn't want to be there and were causing trouble, and the doctor, lawyer, or dentist, without assistance, had to treat them all with professional excellence for nine months, then he might have some conception of the classroom teacher's job.

DONALD D. QUINN

Few things help an individual more than to place responsibility upon him, and to let him know that you trust him.

BOOKER T. WASHINGTON (1856–1915)

Kind words can be short and easy to speak, but their echoes are endless.

MOTHER TERESA (1910–1997)

———

Teachers who act as if they have something to learn as well as something to contribute, establish better learning relationships with students and parents.

ANDY HARGREAVES AND MICHAEL FULLAN
What's Worth Fighting for Out There? (1998)

———

I learned that it is the weak who are cruel, and that gentleness is to be expected only from the strong.

LEO ROSTEN (1909–1997)

Too often we underestimate the power of a touch, a smile, a kind word, a listening ear, an honest compliment, or the smallest act of caring, all of which have the potential to turn a life around.

LEO BUSCAGLIA

Teaching is what teachers expect to do every day. To reach out positively and supportively to twenty-seven youngsters for five hours or so each day in an elementary school classroom is demanding and exhausting. To respond similarly to four to six successive classes of twenty-five or more students each at the secondary level may be impossible.

JOHN GOODLAD
A Place Called School (1984)

A word of encouragement during a failure is worth more than an hour of praise after success.

ANONYMOUS

A decline in the extrinsic payoff requires a compensating improvement in the intrinsic satisfaction of learning if students are to be motivated.

HENRY M. LEVIN
"Back to Basics and the Economy" (1984)

When angry, count ten, before you speak; if very angry, an hundred.

THOMAS JEFFERSON IN A LETTER TO THOMAS JEFFERSON SMITH
(1825)

The benefits gained from learning how to manage conflict constructively far outweighs the costs of learning time lost by students being upset and angry.

THOMAS J. SERGIOVANNI
Building Community in Schools (1994)

It's like being grounded for 18 years.

A NEW YORK CITY BOARD OF EDUCATION POSTER WARNING AGAINST TEEN PREGNANCY (1986)

Let parents then bequeath to their children not riches, but the spirit of reverence.

PLATO
Protagoras (380 B.C.)

You can't hold a man down without staying down with him.

BOOKER T. WASHINGTON (1856–1915)

He allows them their self-respect—indeed, he insists on it.

JAMES BALDWIN
"The Dangerous Road before Martin Luther King" (1961)

When I taught in a public high school for three years I always ate lunch with a different group of students whether they were in my class or not, until I got to know most of them. The teachers thought I was idiotic, but they didn't realize that it actually made it easier for me to teach, that before I could effectively discipline students, I had to earn their friendship and respect.

MARVA COLLINS
Making a Difference in the Classroom (1992)

You can preach at them: that is a hook without a worm; you can order them to volunteer: that is dishonest; you can call upon them: you are needed, and that approach will hardly ever fail.

KURT HAHN (1886–1974)
AS QUOTED IN *Reclaiming Youth at Risk: Our Hope for the Future* (1990)

Children may forget what you say, but they'll never forget how you make them feel.

PARKER J. PALMER

I never reprimand a boy in the evening—darkness and a troubled mind are a poor combination.

FRANK L. BOYDEN
AS QUOTED In *Life* (1962)

I have one rule—attention. They give me theirs and I give them mine.

SISTER EVANGELIST ON TEACHING HIGH SCHOOL STUDENTS
AS QUOTED IN *The Gazette* (1980)

The American male at the peak of his physical powers and appetites, driving 160 big white horses across the scenes of an increasingly open society, with weekend money in his pocket and with little prior exposure to trouble and tragedy, personifies "an accident going to happen."

JOHN SLOAN DICKEY
"Conscience and the Undergraduate" (1955)

Human beings are full of emotion, and the teacher who knows how to use it will have dedicated learners. It means sending dominant signals instead of submissive ones with your eyes, body and voice.

LEON LESSINGER
AS QUOTED IN *Newsweek* (1976)

In communities the best discipline strategies are those that teach students citizenship and help students become caring adults. Key are the standards, values, and commitments that make up a constitution for living together

THOMAS J. SERGIOVANNI
Building Community in Schools (1994)

Obedience is the mother of success, and success the parent of salvation.

AESCHYLUS
The Seven against Thebes (460 B.C.)

It takes time to persuade men to do even what is for their own good.

THOMAS JEFFERSON IN A LETTER TO REVEREND CHARLES CLAY (1790)

No trace of slavery ought to mix with the studies of the freeborn man . . . No study, pursued under compulsion, remains rooted in the memory.

PLATO
The Republic (360 B.C.)

A child cannot be taught by anyone who despises him . . .

JAMES BALDWIN (1912–1987)

Love is at the root of all healthy discipline.

FRED ROGERS
Mister Rogers Talks with Parents (1983)

Be not angry that you cannot make others as you wish them to be, since you cannot make yourself as you wish to be.

THOMAS Á. KEMPIS (1379–1471)

At school Mrs. Dickens liked Paul's picture of the sailboat better than my picture of the invisible castle. At singing time she said I sang too loud. At counting time she said I left out sixteen. Who needs sixteen? I could tell it was going to be a terrible, horrible, no good, very bad day.

JUDITH VIORST
Alexander and the Terrible, Horrible, No Good, Very Bad Day
(1972)

Our earth is degenerate in these latter days; bribery and corruption are common; children no longer obey their parents; and the end of the world is evidently approaching.

ASSYRIAN CLAY TABLET (2800 B.C.)

It's not their fault they're slugs.

THE MACOMBER SISTERS

8

Those We Teach

Everyone is somebody's child . . .

Father, mother, sister, brother. Singer, dancer, cynic, romancer. Fireman, venture capitalist, contractor, environmentalist. Rabbi, priest, giver of love, taker of grief. Farm hand, astronaut, drinker of whiskey, smoker of pot.

Super husband and perfect wife, doer of good and victim of life. Rainbow dreamer and counterfeit schemer, juggler of knives and driver of Beemer. Writer and undertaker, butcher and baker. The candlestick maker.

Picker of fruit and maid to the banker, short-order cook on an ill-fated tanker. TV evangelist, paralegal, waitress at the Regal Beagle. Olympic gymnast and backyard gardener, biographer of Ring Lardner. Graphic artist and auto mechanic, medicated outpatient in perpetual panic. Police officer and big city cabbie, small town version of *Dear Abby*. Guidance counselor and heroin addict, Oakland Raiders football fanatic. Insurance salesman and thespian, late night stand-up comedian.

... just as they were once somebody's student.

Adults are obsolete children.

DR. SEUSS (1904–1991)

The chief cause of human errors is to be found in the prejudices picked up in childhood.

RENÉ DESCARTES (1596–1650)

Education commences at the mother's knee, and every word spoken within the hearing of little children tends towards the formation of character

HOSEA BALLOU (1771–1853)

The potential possibilities of any child are the most intriguing and stimulating in all creation.

RAY L. WILBUR (1875–1949)

They come to me without an inkling of what talent and power of perception they have . . . and very rarely has anyone ever bothered to credit their insight.

LENNI ABEL
ART TEACHER AND 2000 DISNEY "TEACHER OF THE YEAR" FROM THE BRONX

Good teachers empathize with kids, respect them, and believe that each one has something special that can be built upon.

ANN LIEBERMAN

We worry about what a child will be tomorrow, yet we forget that he or she is someone today.

STACIA TAUSHER

Child, give me your hand that I may walk in the light of your faith in me.

HANNAH KAHN

Every day we wake up and we're the same as we were when we fell asleep, but we look into the mirror and see two faces. One face is ours and the other face is what our minds make up for us, sort of like a fantasy. There is no reason why we can't accept who we are. We are who we are for a reason. But we all want to be different in one way or another. We judge, and we get judged. We make stereotypes for no reason at all and sometimes not even on purpose. We are tough, and we are weak. We are beautiful and ugly. We see things differently. We do things differently. And we look different. There is no normal, but we all cry and we all dream the same . . .

BRIAN CALLABRO
P/NW BOCES CULINARY ARTS ACADEMY (2001)

Our errors are surely not such awfully solemn things. In a world where we are so certain to incur them in spite of all our caution, a certain lightness of heart seems healthier than this excessive nervousness on their behalf.

WILLIAM JAMES
"The Will to Believe" (1897)

To be alienated is to lack a sense of belonging, to feel cut off from family, friends, school or work—the four worlds of childhood.

URI BRONFENBRENNER
AS QUOTED IN THE *Phi Delta Kappan* (1986)

A cynical young person is almost the saddest sight to see, because it means that he or she has gone from knowing nothing to believing in nothing.

MAYA ANGELOU (1928–)

Children are liquid. They shape themselves to fit the form of the container into which they are placed . . . I am forever indebted to my teachers. They had enough faith to swing the bucket, because they knew that it was in the very nature of the water to remain right there.

PAULA POLK LILLARD
Montessori Today: A Comprehensive Approach to Education from Birth to Adulthood (1996)

There is always one moment in childhood when the door opens and lets the future in.

GRAHAM GREENE
The Power and the Glory (1940)

———

Spring, spring is here at last
And now, and now
We can run through the grass
We can jump
We can sing
We can do anything
We can kiss and hug
A little black bug
Oh Spring, oh Spring is here at last!

MELISSA BROOKS KELLY, A NINE-YEAR-OLD
IN *Wee Wisdom* (1978)

Children's talent to endure stems from their ignorance of alternatives.

MAYA ANGELOU
I Know Why the Caged Bird Sings (1969)

———•——•———

I have often wondered about two things. First, why high-school kids almost invariably hate the books they are assigned to read by their English teachers, and second, why English teachers almost invariably hate the books their students read in their spare time.

STEPHEN KING
"What Stephen King Does For Love" IN *Seventeen* (1990)

Kids today are oriented to immediacy. Theirs is a world of fast foods, fast music, fast cars, fast relationships and fast gratification. They are not buying our promise for tomorrow because they don't think we can deliver, and they are probably right.

LeRoy E. Hay
1983 NATIONAL "TEACHER OF THE YEAR"

Sometimes parents require new teachers to earn their trust. They view us as experimenting with their kid. If you show them you really care, then they are supportive.

MIKE BENEVENTO TEACHER IN UPPER SADDLE RIVER, NEW JERSEY
AS QUOTED IN *"Survival Guide for New Teachers"* (2000)

I believe that the individual who is to be educated is a social individual, and that the society is an organic union of individuals. If we eliminate the social factor from the child we are left only with an abstraction; if we eliminate the individual factor from society, we are left only with an inert and lifeless mass.

JOHN DEWEY (1859–1952)
AS QUOTED IN *John Dewey on Education* (1964)

It is important that students bring a certain ragamuffin, barefoot irreverence to their studies; they are not here to worship what is known, but to question it.

JACOB BRONOWSKI

Let the potential artist in our children come to life that they may surmount industrial monotonies and pressures.

BARBARA MORGAN

⸻

There is no such thing as a weird human being. It's just that some people require more understanding than others do.

TOM ROBBINS
Another Roadside Attraction (1971)

We forget that with some natures it is necessary to train the individual, and to develop his or her special abilities: such people may never be absorbed into any group, and yet be of great service to themselves and to mankind.

GILBERT HIGHET ON ALBERT SCHWEITZER
The Immortal Profession (1976)

Children and adults alike share needs to be safe and secure; to belong and to be loved; to experience self-esteem through achievement, mastery, recognition, and respect; to be autonomous; and to experience self-actualization by pursuing one's inner abilities and finding intrinsic meaning and satisfaction in what one does.

THOMAS J. SERGIOVANNI
Building Community in Schools (1994)

Schools are to prepare the young for the future, for earthly conditions as they will be, not as they were, for manhood appropriate to a future rather than to a present time, for values relevant to the inevitably changing conditions that will obtain two or four or more decades hence.

THEODORE R. SIZER
Places for Learning, Places for Joy: Speculations on American School Reform (1973)

The public schools are America's children and require the continuing encouragement, nurture, and support of America's people.

IRA SINGER
"What's the Real Point of a Nation at Risk?"

Respect for the fragility and importance of an individual life is still the first mark of an educated man.

NORMAN COUSINS (1915–1990)

Awareness need never remain superficial in an educated man, whereas unawareness is certain to be ignorance probably compounded by arrogance.

NATIONAL CONFERENCE ON HIGHER EDUCATION (1964)

The intellectual development of the child is no clockwork sequence of events; it also responds to influences from the environment, notably the school environment.

JEROME S. BRUNER (1915–)
AS QUOTED IN *The Teacher and the Taught* (1963)

I am old-fashioned and romantic enough to believe that many children, given the right circumstances, are natural readers until this instinct is destroyed by the media. It may be an illusion to believe that the magical connection of solitary children to the best books can endure, but such a relationship does go so long a way back that it will not easily expire.

HAROLD BLOOM
Short Stories and Poems for Exceptionally Intelligent Children (2001)

Reading, in contrast to sitting before the screen, is not a purely passive exercise. The child, particularly one who reads a book dealing with real life, has nothing before it but the hieroglyphics of the printed page. Imagination must do the rest; and imagination is called upon to do it.

GEORGE F. KENNAN
"American Addictions" IN THE *New Oxford Review* (1993)

Whether you are a middle-class suburbanite, a parent living in the slums of a major city or a resident of a rural area, your involvement will mean that your child will learn more and do better in school.

MELITTA J. CUTRIGHT
The National PTA Talks to Parents: How to Get the Best Education for Your Child (1989)

Many theorists have written about education as if it were chiefly intended to teach young people to live in society. Yet it is clear, when we look at young men and women, that they also need to be taught how to live with themselves.

GILBERT HIGHET
The Immortal Profession (1976)

If it be urged that some men have such weak intellects that it is not possible for them to acquire knowledge, I answer that it is scarcely possible to find a mirror so dulled that it will not reflect images of some kind, or for a tablet to have such a rough surface that nothing can be inscribed on it.

JOHN AMOS COMENIUS (1592–1670)
AS QUOTED IN *The Teacher and the Taught* (1963)

Every child's life is like a piece of paper on which every person leaves a mark.

CHINESE PROVERB

Young people need much more to be demanded of them. They need to be needed, they need to give, they need opportunities to show love, courage, sacrifice. They need to be part of a cause that is larger than the sum of their individual appetites. They need to believe in something.

THOMAS SOBOL IN HIS CLOSING ADDRESS TO THE SUMMER LAW INSTITUTE AT COLUMBIA UNIVERSITY (2000)

I had learned to respect the intelligence, integrity, creativity and capacity for deep thought and hard work latent somewhere in every child; they had learned that I differed from them only in years and experience, and that as I, an ordinary human being, loved and respected them, I expected payment in kind.

SYBIL MARSHALL ON EIGHTEEN YEARS AS TEACHER IN A ONE-ROOM SCHOOL IN ENGLAND
An Experiment in Education (1963)

Teenagers go to college to be with their boyfriends and girlfriends; they go because they can't think of anything else to do; they go because their parents want them to and sometimes because their parents don't want them to; they go to find themselves, or to find a husband, or to get away from home, and sometimes even to find out about the world in which they live.

HAROLD HOWE II
AS QUOTED IN *Newsweek* (1976)

We save a boy's soul at the same time we are saving his algebra.

GEORGE C. ST. JOHN, RECALLED AT HIS FUNERAL (1966)

What I'm concerned about is the people who *don't* dwell on the meaninglessness of their lives, or the meaningfulness of it—who just pursue mindless entertainment.

MICHAEL K. HOOKER
AS QUOTED IN THE *Christian Science Monitor* (1986)

I see the mind of the five-year-old as a volcano with two vents: destructiveness and creativeness.

SYLVIA ASHTON-WARNER
Teacher (1963)

Genius, when young, is divine.

BENJAMIN DISRAELI
Coningsby (1844)

No one can keep a secret better than a child.

VICTOR HUGO
Les Misérables (1862)

Children have never been very good at listening to their elders, but they have never failed to imitate them.

JAMES BALDWIN
Nobody Knows My Name (1961)

Your children are not your children. They are the sons and daughters of Life's longing for itself. They came through you but not from you. And though they are with you yet they belong not to you. You may give them your love but not your thoughts, for they have their own thoughts.

> KHALIL GIBRAN
> *The Prophet* (1923)

I cannot think of any need in childhood as strong as the need for a father's protection.

> SIGMUND FREUD
> *Civilization and Its Discontents* (1931)

... if this world were anything near what it should be there would be no more need of a Book Week than there would be of a Society for the Prevention of Cruelty to Children.

DOROTHY PARKER (1893–1967)
AS QUOTED IN *Constant Reader* (1928)

So long as little children are allowed to suffer, there is no true love in this world.

ISADORA DUNCAN (1878–1927)
AS QUOTED IN *This Quarter* (1929)

I long remained a child, and I am still one in many respects.

JEAN JACQUES ROUSSEAU
Confessions, Book Four (1782)

Such, such were the joys
When we all, girls and boys
In our youth time were seen
On the Echoing Green.

WILLIAM BLAKE
Songs of the Innocence (1789)

9

The Motivational and the Inspirational

Here are a few of the things that inspire me most.

. . . cresting the concrete horizon at Yankee Stadium to be embraced by green, green grass and the rich brown of the infield dirt, raked to perfection; watching the lazy calisthenics in the outfield as I slide down the aisle to my seat; hearing the smack of leather on leather and Bob Shepherd's voice with the day's line-ups. All of this before the game even starts, a world of possibilities just one "Star Spangled Banner" away.

. . . the Tuesday I've been waiting for finally comes. After work, I drive to the music store, go straight to the New Releases rack, and rip off the wrapping before starting the car again. The sound my favorite band has been secretly cultivating for months now is pouring from my speakers. The album is mine. I find it hard to keep from speeding, not because I want to get home any faster than usual but because my heart is pumping as hard as each successive beat.

. . . settling down with a book and not realizing that the first hundred pages have already passed me by. If

I'm lying in the hammock or rocking back and forth in front of the fireplace, all the better. I don't mind missing the characters once the book is finished because I know two things: one, there are other characters out there, just waiting to be discovered and two, the characters I'm leaving behind will always be there if I choose to return.

. . . the feeling of relief that comes with finally writing *the* sentence. There is such anxiety attached to the idea of someone reading my words, especially when what I'm writing is important to me. But it is this sharing that makes the struggle so worthwhile. To be able to write a sentence that resonates is one of the most satisfying feelings in the world.

. . . by the same token, hearing a student say, "I didn't think I'd be able to do it." Or, "I never knew that." Like the ball off of the bat or the first lyric of the first song, this brings incredible excitement and joy. The look in that child's eye, it's better than the Yankees winning or the book ending in an unexpected manner, just as I wanted it to all along. Each student is a chapter in the greatest story I could ever hope to write. It is this that inspires me most.

———

Language is a living, kicking, growing, flitting, evolving reality, and the teacher should spontaneously reflect its vibrant and protean qualities.

JOHN A. RASSIAS
AS QUOTED IN *Quote* (1974)

———

No act of kindness, no matter how small, is ever wasted.

AESOP (SIXTH CENTURY B.C.?)

Nurture your minds with great thoughts. To believe in the heroic makes heroes.

BENJAMIN DISRAELI (1804–1881)

As your body grows bigger
Your mind must flower
It's great to learn
'cause knowledge is power!

TOM YOHE
FROM ABC'S SATURDAY MORNING PUBLIC SERVICE CAMPAIGN,
"Schoolhouse Rock"

We are the inheritors of a past that gives us every reason to believe that we will succeed.

A Nation at Risk: The Full Account EDITED BY USA RESEARCH
(1983)

My heart is singing for joy . . . The light of understanding has shone in my little pupil's mind, and behold, all things are changed.

ANNE SULLIVAN (1866–1936)

You don't have to be tall to see the moon.

AFRICAN PROVERB

The future is yet full of trial and success. There is happiness to be enjoyed! There is good to be done! Exchange this false life of thine for a true one.

NATHANIEL HAWTHORNE (1804–1864)

Education breeds confidence. Confidence breeds hope. Hope breeds peace.

CONFUCIUS (C. 551–479 B.C.)

The best teachers give their pupils both a sense of order, discipline, control; and a powerful stimulus which urges them to take their destinies in their own hands, kick over rules, and transgress all boundaries.

GILBERT HIGHET
The Immortal Profession (1976)

Life isn't about finding yourself. Life is about creating yourself.

GEORGE BERNARD SHAW (1856–1950)

If you rest, you rust.

HELEN HAYES
My Life in Three Acts (1990)

Education is the power to think clearly, the power to act well in the world's work, and the power to appreciate life.

BRIGHAM YOUNG (1801–1877)

Nurture your mind with great thoughts, for you will never go any higher than you think.

BENJAMIN DISRAELI (1804–1881)

Knowledge is not simply another commodity. On the contrary. Knowledge is never used up. It increases by diffusion and grows by dispersion.

DANIEL J. BOORSTIN TO THE HOUSE APPROPRIATIONS SUBCOMMITTEE
AS QUOTED IN *The New York Times* (1986)

Even if I knew that tomorrow the world would go to pieces, I would still plant my apple tree.

MARTIN LUTHER (1483–1546)

Genius is one percent inspiration, ninety-nine percent perspiration.

THOMAS A. EDISON IN 1903 AND QUOTED IN *Harper's* (1932)

If you want to increase your success rate, double your failure rate.

> THOMAS WATSON, SR.
> FOUNDER OF IBM

Make a true estimate of your own ability, then raise it ten percent.

> NORMAN VINCENT PEALE (1898–1993)

Life is ten percent what happens to me and ninety percent how I react to it.

> CHARLES SWINDOLL

The circumstances that surround a man's life are not important. How that man responds to those circumstances is important. His response is the ultimate determining factor between success and failure.

BOOKER T. WASHINGTON (1856–1915)

When the One Great Scorer comes to write against
   your name
He marks not that you won or lost
But how you played the game.

GRANTLAND RICE (1880–1954)

Education is not to reform students or amuse them or to make them expert technicians. It is to unsettle their minds, widen their horizons, inflame their intellects, teach them to think straight, if possible.

ROBERT M. HUTCHINS ON ACADEMIC FREEDOM
AS QUOTED IN *Time* (1952)

———

Yesterday is a dream, tomorrow but a vision. But today well lived makes every yesterday a dream of happiness, and every tomorrow a vision of hope. Look well, therefore, to this day.

SANSKRIT PROVERB

———

Teaching is the most inherently hopeful act that I know of.

PATRICIA MURPHY, TEACHER FROM OTTAWA
AS QUOTED IN *What's Worth Fighting for Out There?* (1998)

I don't know what your destiny will be, but one thing I know: the only ones among you who will be truly happy are those who will have sought and found how to serve.

ALBERT SCHWEITZER (1875–1965)

When you do a thing, do it with all your might. Put your whole soul into it. Stamp it with your own personality . . . Nothing great was ever achieved without enthusiasm.

RALPH WALDO EMERSON (1803–1882)

Knowledge is the eye of desire and can become the pilot of the soul.

WILL DURANT (1885–1981)

Reflect upon your present blessings, of which every man has plenty; not on your past misfortunes, of which all men have some.

CHARLES DICKENS (1812–1870)

The great tragedy of life doesn't lie in failing to reach your goals. The great tragedy lies in having no goals to reach.

BENJAMIN E. MAYS (1894–1984)

AS QUOTED BY MARIAN WRIGHT EDELMAN IN *The New York Times* (1985)

Robert E. Lee didn't make it the first time and Jefferson Davis took the vacancy. Pershing didn't make it for two years, MacArthur couldn't get in the first year and Eisenhower took an extra year of high school to get in. [Patton] took three years to get in and five to get out.

MANLEY E. ROGERS ON SOME OF WEST POINT'S MORE FAMOUS CADETS
AS QUOTED IN *The New York Times* (1985)

We must accept finite disappointment, but we must never lose infinite hope.

MARTIN LUTHER KING, JR. (1929–1968)

Strength does not come from physical capacity. It comes from an indomitable will.

MAHATMA GANDHI (1869–1948)

A teacher affects eternity; he can never tell where his influence stops.

HENRY B. ADAMS (1838–1918)

The teacher is one who makes two ideas grow where only one grew before.

ELBERT HUBBARD (1856–1915)

Education is not filling a bucket, but lighting a fire.

WILLIAM YEATS (1865–1939)

He would not be ashamed of dying . . . He could be research. A human textbook. *Study me in my slow and patient demise. Watch what happens to me. Learn with me.*

MITCH ALBOM
Tuesdays with Morrie (1997)

I am only one; but still I am one. I cannot do everything, but still I can do something. I will not refuse to do the something I can do.

HELEN KELLER (1880–1968)

Anything one man can imagine, other men can make real.

JULES VERNE (1828–1905)

Imagination is more important than knowledge.

ALBERT EINSTEIN (1879–1955)

On a good day, I know it's not every day, we can part
   the sea
And on a bad day, I know it's not every day, glory
   beyond our reach.

CHRIS ROBINSON
"Wiser Time" (1994)

What lies behind us and what lies before us are tiny
matters compared to what lies within us.

OLIVER WENDELL HOLMES (1841–1935)

I respect faith, but doubt is what gets you an education.

WILSON MIZNER (1876–1933)

AS QUOTED IN *The Legendary Mizners* BY ALVA JOHNSTON (1953)

When love and skill work together, expect a masterpiece.

JOHN RUSKIN (1819–1900)

As long as you live, keep learning how to live.

LUCIUS ANNAEUS SENECA (C. 4 B.C.–65 A.D.)

It is good even for old men to learn wisdom.

AESCHYLUS
Fragments

I put the relation of a fine teacher to a student just below the relation of a mother to a son . . .

THOMAS WOLFE (1900–1938)

Employ your time in improving yourself by other men's writings, so that you shall gain easily what others have labored hard for.

SOCRATES (469–399 B.C.)

When inspiration does not come to me, I go halfway to meet it.

SIGMUND FREUD (1856–1939)

If you can dream it you can do it.

WALT DISNEY (1901–1966)

I do not teach children, I give them joy.

ISADORA DUNCAN (1878–1927)

From what we get, we can make a living; what we give, however, makes a life.

ARTHUR ASHE (1943–1993)

Don't judge each day by the harvest you reap, but by the seeds you plant.

ROBERT LOUIS STEVENSON (1850–1894)

Try to learn something about everything and everything about something.

THOMAS HUXLEY (1825–1895)

Education happens when hope exceeds expectation.

ANDY HARGREAVES AND MICHAEL FULLAN
What's Worth Fighting for Out There? (1998)

I love to see a young girl go out and grab the world by the lapels.

MAYA ANGELOU
Girl about Town (1986)

When the uncapped potential of a student meets the liberating art of a teacher, a miracle unfolds.

MARY HATWOOD FUTRELL

Talent builds itself in stillness, character in the stream of the world.

JOHANN WOLFGANG VON GOETHE (1749–1832)
AS QUOTED IN *The Immortal Profession* (1976)

———

You always pass failure on the road to success.

MICKEY ROONEY (1920–)

———

Sometimes one man with courage is a majority.

ANDREW JACKSON (1767–1845)

I know of no more encouraging fact than the unquestionable ability of man to elevate his life by conscious endeavor.

HENRY DAVID THOREAU (1817–1862)

No matter what accomplishments you achieve, somebody helped you.

ALTHEA GIBSON (1927–)
AS QUOTED IN *WomenSports* (1976)

All growth is a leap in the dark.

HENRY MILLER (1891–1980)

Work 'em hard, play 'em hard, feed 'em up to the nines and send 'em to bed so tired that they are asleep before their heads are on the pillow.

FRANK L. BOYDEN
AS QUOTED IN *News Summaries* (1954)

The very least you can do in your life is to figure out what you hope for. And the most you can do is live inside that hope. Not admire it from a distance but live right in it, under its roof.

BARBARA KINGSOLVER
Animal Dreams (1997)

Many great actions are committed in small struggles.

VICTOR HUGO
Les Misérables (1862)

Far and away the best prize that life offers is the chance to work hard at work worth doing.

THEODORE ROOSEVELT IN A LABOR DAY SPEECH (1903)

Seek knowledge from the cradle to the grave.

MUHAMMAD (571?–634? A.D.)

We may have all come on different ships, but we're in the same boat now.

MARTIN LUTHER KING, JR. (1929–1968)

From the Agreeable to the Outright Laughable

One of the reasons I teach has absolutely nothing to do with a higher cause or any of that business. And no, it isn't the summer vacations! It's the fact that I love to laugh. My students give me this gift.

There's plenty of humility: "Is that your daughter, Mr. Howe?" a third grader asks as he looks at my wedding picture.

Attention-grabbing announcements: "Mr. Howe, I'm not doin' any work today!" a teen mother tells me as she arrives to class five minutes early.

Even fashion criticisms: "Hey Mr. Howe, the 1970s called . . . They want their belt back."

These kids also give me a different type of gift. Believe it or not, it is from them that I am granted pause in the torrent of the day—a reflective pause stemming from a "Guess what I heard?" or a "Did you know?" Oftentimes, I hadn't heard; I didn't know. As they move away from me, walking down the hall toward the gym or the cafeteria or the busses, I am left with another warm memory.

Whether they are making me laugh, or simply nod my head in agreement, the common denominator is the truth. I am constantly thankful for these gifts. They are honesty in its purest form.

The price of your hat isn't the measure of your brain.

AFRICAN-AMERICAN PROVERB

His test scores, for general aptitude, showed that he wasn't very apt at anything; he was no natural. This came as no surprise to Garp, who shared with his mother a belief that *nothing* came naturally.

JOHN IRVING
The World According to Garp (1978)

If I were asked to enumerate ten educational stupidities, the giving of grades would head the list . . . If I can't give a child a better reason for studying than a grade on a report card, I ought to lock my desk and go home and stay there

DOROTHY DE ZOUCHE

You go to school, you get a master's degree, you study Shakespeare and you wind up being famous for plastic glasses.

SALLY JESSY RAPHAEL (1943–)

Equality is not when a female Einstein gets promoted to assistant professor. Equality is when a female schlemiel moves ahead as fast as a male schlemiel.

EWALD B. NYQUIST
AS QUOTED IN *The New York Times* (1975)

I think I am, therefore, I am. I think.

GEORGE CARLIN
Napalm and Silly Putty (2001)

Why are there five syllables in the word "monosyllabic"? And how come "abbreviated" is such a long word?

STEVEN WRIGHT

Is sloppiness in speech caused by ignorance or apathy? I don't know and I don't care.

WILLIAM SAFIRE (1929–)

Shortchange your education now and you may be short of change the rest of your life.

ANONYMOUS

If the teacher said on the report card, *This kid is a total and hopeless jackass who may have trouble learning his zip code,* then the parent wouldn't be teased by the possibility of scholastic success.

BILL COSBY
Fatherhood (1987)

A gifted teacher is as rare as a gifted doctor, and makes far less money.

ANONYMOUS

Education seems to be in America the only commodity of which the customer tries to get as little as he can for his money.

MAX FORMAN

Education costs money, but so does ignorance.

SIR CLAUDE MOSER

In America the young are always ready to give to those who are older than themselves the full benefits of their inexperience.

OSCAR WILDE
"The American Invasion" IN *Court and Society Review* (1887)

My father must have had some elementary education for he could read and write and keep accounts inaccurately.

GEORGE BERNARD SHAW (1856–1950)

Television commercials are educational. They teach you how stupid advertisers think you are.

ANONYMOUS

You can lead a boy to college, but you cannot make him think.

ELBERT HUBBARD (1856–1915)

Knowledge is good.

EMIL FABER
FROM *"Animal House"* (1978)

Coach Spence taught in the upbeat, vibrant manner of a coach and was energetic in a way that made you pay attention. He also related moments in history to quotes from movies like *The Blues Brothers*. Classic!

JEREMY HOGERSON, MAMARONECK HIGH SCHOOL '90 (2002)

Whenever you asked him how he was doing in school, he always said, "No problem." And his answer made sense: there *was* no problem, no confusion about how he was doing. He had failed everything; and what he hadn't failed, he hadn't taken yet.

BILL COSBY
Fatherhood (1987)

SUGGESTED BUMPER STICKER: We Are the Proud Parents of a Child Whose Self-Esteem Is Sufficient that He Doesn't Need Us Advertising His Minor Scholastic Achievement on the Bumper of Our Car.

GEORGE CARLIN
Napalm and Silly Putty (2001)

Anyone who stops learning is old, whether twenty or eighty. Anyone who keeps learning today is young. The greatest thing in life is to keep your mind young.

HENRY FORD (1863–1947)

The sound that best describes teaching is the sound of a car being driven by someone just learning how to drive a stick shift. It's getting somewhere, but nowhere quickly, and there are a lot of stops and starts in between.

MARGARET STRUHAR
ENGLISH TEACHER IN YORKTOWN HEIGHTS, NEW YORK (2002)

Teachers are sometimes thought of as respectable drudges—like hospital nurses, or even like attendants in an asylum for the harmless insane.

GILBERT HIGHET
The Immortal Profession (1976)

Few statements on quality education deal with teachers' needs in day-to-day school operation. Teachers, apparently, are taken for granted as a part of the classroom scenery, like desks, chairs, and books.

J. LLOYD TRUMP (1908–)
AS QUOTED IN *The Teacher and the Taught* (1963)

Education is when you read the fine print. Experience is what you get if you don't.

PETE SEEGER (1919–)

If ignorance is bliss, there should be more happy people.

VICTOR COUSINS

Why doesn't glue stick to the inside of the bottle?

STEVEN WRIGHT

Life is a festival only to the wise.

RALPH WALDO EMERSON (1803–1882)

Be wiser than other people if you can; but do not tell them so.

LORD CHESTERFIELD

It is best for the wise man not to seem wise.

AESCHYLUS
Prometheus Bound (430 B.C.)

———

I was thrown out of NYU my freshman year . . . for cheating on my metaphysics final. You know, I looked within the soul of the boy sitting next to me.

WOODY ALLEN
Annie Hall (1977)

———

When you think about it, attention deficit disorder makes a lot of sense. In this country there isn't a lot worth paying attention to.

GEORGE CARLIN
Napalm and Silly Putty (2001)

Analysts of the American psyche may explain that we pick particularly on the schools when we're unhappy with ourselves . . .

THEODORE R. SIZER (1932–)

Love truth, but pardon error.

VOLTAIRE
Discours sur l'Homme

Parents may tell
But never teach
Unless they practice
What they preach.

ANONYMOUS

If nobody said anything unless he knew what he was talking about, a ghastly hush would descend upon the earth.

SIR ALAN HERBERT (1890–1971)

I have never let my schooling interfere with my education.

MARK TWAIN (1835–1910)

If there were no schools to take the children away from home part of the time, the insane asylum would be filled with mothers.

EDGAR WATSON HOWE (1853–1937)

Just think of the tragedy of teaching children not to doubt.

CLARENCE DARROW (1857–1938)

The vanity of teaching often tempteth a man to forget he is a blockhead.

GEORGE SAVILE

There are two ways to slide easily through life: to believe everything or to doubt everything. Both ways save us from thinking.

ALFRED KORZYBSKI (1879–1950)

Wisdom is as the moon rises, perceptible not in progress but in result.

<small>CHINESE PROVERB</small>

Education is . . . hanging around until you've caught on.

<small>ROBERT FROST (1874–1963)</small>

One of the greatest problems of our time is that many are schooled but few are educated.

<small>THOMAS MOORE (1779–1852)</small>

Garp knew what to take for courses and whom to have for teachers. That is often the difference between doing well or poorly in a school. He was not really a gifted student, but he had direction.

JOHN IRVING
The World According to Garp (1978)

Whose cruel idea was it for the word "lisp" to have an "s" in it?

STEVEN WRIGHT

It is nobler to be good, and it is nobler to teach others to be good—and less trouble!

MARK TWAIN (1835–1910)

Praise does wonders for our sense of hearing.

ARNOLD H. GLASGOW

The mind is more vulnerable than the stomach, because it can be poisoned without feeling immediate pain.

HELEN MacINNES (1907–1985)

When you stack up the years we are allowed against all there is to read, time is very short indeed.

STEPHEN KING
"What Stephen King Does for Love" IN *Seventeen* (1990)

If you see two children, one of whom is clean and the other is dirty, you tend to suppose that the clean one's parents have a larger income than the parents of the dirty one. Consequently snobs try to keep their children very clean. This is an abominable tyranny which interferes with the children doing a great many of the things they had better be doing.

BERTRAND RUSSELL (1872–1970)
AS QUOTED IN *The Teacher and the Taught* (1963)

Men dress their children's minds as they do their bodies, in the prevailing fashion.

HERBERT SPENCER (1820–1903)
AS QUOTED IN *The Teacher and the Taught* (1963)

You can pay people to teach, but you can't pay them to care.

MARVA COLLINS
Making a Difference in the Classroom (1992)

Everyone is ignorant, only on different subjects.

WILL ROGERS (1879–1935)

How is it that little children are so intelligent and men so stupid? It must be education that does it.

ALEXANDRE DUMAS (1802–1870)

It is bad enough to see young fools, but worse to see old fools.

BRIGHAM YOUNG (1801–1877)

He was so learned that he could name a horse in nine languages; so ignorant that he bought a cow to ride on.

BENJAMIN FRANKLIN
Poor Richard's Almanac (1758)

Teaching for tests creates learnoids.

ALAN SCOTT WINSTON

Our metaphors arise from the factory floor and issue from the military manual. Education, apparently, is something someone does to somebody else.

THEODORE R. SIZER
Horace's Compromise (1984)

Compromise is fine for people who aren't as right as me.

ESMÉ RAJI CODELL
Educating Esmé (1999)

As for helping me in the outside world, the Convent taught me only that if you spit on a pencil eraser, it will erase ink.

DOROTHY PARKER ON PAROCHIAL SCHOOL (WHICH SHE ATTENDED
UNTIL SHE WAS ASKED TO LEAVE AT AGE THIRTEEN) (1893–1967)

It is better to ask some of the questions than know all of the answers.

JAMES THURBER (1894–1961)

He who is ashamed of asking is ashamed of learning.

DANISH PROVERB

I was gratified to be able to answer promptly. I said I didn't know.

MARK TWAIN (1835–1910)

Start a program for gifted children, and every parent demands that his child be enrolled.

THOMAS BAILEY
AS QUOTED IN THE *Wall Street Journal* (1961)

If you promise not to believe everything your child says happens at this school, I'll promise not to believe everything he says happens at home.

A NOTE TO STUDENTS' PARENTS FROM AN ENGLISH SCHOOLMASTER
AS QUOTED IN THE *Wall Street Journal* (1985)

The only reason I always try to meet and know the parents better is because it helps me to forgive their children.

LOUIS JOHANNOT
AS QUOTED IN *Life* (1965)

It is indeed ironic that we spend our school days yearning to graduate and our remaining days waxing nostalgic about our school days.

ISABEL WAXMAN

Teaching is not a lost art, but the regard for it is a lost tradition.

JACQUES BARZUN (1907–)
AS QUOTED IN *Newsweek* (1955)

To be loose with grammar is to be loose with the worst woman in the world.

OTIS C. EDWARDS IN A LECTURE AT NASHOTAH HOUSE EPISCOPAL SEMINARY (1966)

We have inadvertently designed a system in which being good at what you do as a teacher is not formally rewarded, while being poor at what you do is seldom corrected nor penalized.

ELLIOT EISNER
AS QUOTED IN *The New York Times* (1985)

———

Anyone who refuses to speak out off campus does not deserve to be listened to on campus.

THEODORE M. HESBURGH (1917–)
AS QUOTED IN *The New York Times* (1984)

———

At college age, you can tell who is best at taking tests and going to school, but you can't tell who the best people are. That worries the hell out of me.

BARNABY C. KEENEY, RECALLED ON HIS DEATH (1980)

Ignorant people in preppy clothes are more dangerous to America than oil embargoes.

V. S. NAIPAUL AFTER A YEAR OF TEACHING AT WESLEYAN UNIVERSITY AS QUOTED IN *Time* (1979)

The University of Miami is not a campus with visible school spirit, just visible tan lines.

LISA BIRNBACH
LISA BIRNBACH'S COLLEGE BOOK (1984)

They wanted a great university without building a great university. They knew a lot about football, but not a lot about academia.

BRAD CARTER ON THE NCAA'S SUSPENSION OF SOUTHERN METHODIST UNIVERSITY'S FOOTBALL PROGRAM, AS QUOTED IN *The New York Times* (1987)

Minerva House ... was "a finishing establishment for young ladies," where some twenty girls of the ages from thirteen to nineteen inclusive, acquired a smattering of everything and a knowledge of nothing.

CHARLES DICKENS
Sketches by Boz (1835)

He ketched a frog one day and took him home and said he cal'lated to educate him; and so he never done nothing for three months but set in his back yard and learn that frog to jump ... He'd give him a little punch behind, and the next minute you'd see that frog whirling in the air like a doughnut ... Smiley said all a frog wanted was education, and he could do most anything—and I believe him.

MARK TWAIN
"The Notorious Jumping Frog of Calaveras County" (1875)

I am afraid we must make the world honest before we can honestly say to our children that honesty is the best policy.

GEORGE BERNARD SHAW (1856–1950)
AS QUOTED DURING A RADIO BROADCAST (1932)

For God's sake give me the young man who has brains enough to make a fool of himself!

ROBERT LOUIS STEVENSON
"Crabbed Age and Youth" (1881)

Winter is the time for study, you know, and the colder it is the more studious we are.

HENRY DAVID THOREAU IN A LETTER TO SOPHIA THOREAU (1847)

Wit is educated insolence.

ARISTOTLE
The Art of Rhetoric

———•·•·•———

The secret of teaching is to appear to have known all your life what you just learned this morning.

ANONYMOUS

———•·•·•———

Microscopes and telescopes really confuse our minds.

JOHANN WOLFGANG VON GOETHE
Reflections in the Spirit of the Travelers (1829)

A fellow declaring he's no fool usually has his suspicions.

WILSON MIZNER (1876–1933)
AS QUOTED IN *The Legendary Mizners* (1953)

———

What we want is to see the child in pursuit of knowledge, and not knowledge in pursuit of the child.

GEORGE BERNARD SHAW (1856–1950)

———

I would be most content if my children grew up to be the kind of people who think decorating consists mostly of building enough bookshelves.

ANNA QUINDLEN

Children seldom misquote you. In fact, they usually repeat word for word what you shouldn't have said.

ANONYMOUS

Biographies

Abigail Adams (1744–1818): Wife of United States president John and mother of United States president John Quincy. Her letters are chronicled in *The Adams-Jefferson Letters* and *The New Letters of Abigail Adams.*

Franklin P. Adams (1881–1960): American journalist.

Henry B. Adams (1838–1918): Historian, journalist, and professor of medieval history at Harvard (1870–1877); grandson of John Quincy.

John Adams (1735–1826): Second president of the United States (1797–1801); husband of Abigail and father of John Quincy.

Joseph Addison (1672–1719): English essayist and politician.

Mortimer J. Adler (1902–2001): Student of John Dewey; professor of education at Columbia University; developed the Paideia Program (a plan for the reform of public schools); author of *The Great Ideas: A Lexicon of Western Thought.*

Aeschylus (c. 525–c. 456 B.C.): Greek playwright known as the "father of tragedies."

Aesop (sixth century B.C.?): Legendary Greek author of fables including "The Tortoise and the Hare" and "The Ant and the Grasshopper."

Mitch Albom (1958–): Author of the best-selling *Tuesdays with Morrie;* sports journalist (newspapers, radio, television).

Amos Bronson Alcott (1799–1888): Educator, social reformer, and author; opened Temple School in Boston; superintendent of schools in Concord; father of author, Louisa May.

Woody Allen (1935–): Actor, writer, and Academy Award–winning director of *Annie Hall*.

Henri Frédéric Amiel (1821–1881): Swiss philosopher and writer.

Sherwood Anderson (1876–1941): Author best known for *Winesburg, Ohio*; consumed with man's struggles in the industrialized world.

Maya Angelou (1928–): African-American writer, educator, historian, civil-rights activist, director, and singer; author of the autobiographical *I Know Why the Caged Bird Sings*.

Jerold W. Apps: Author of *Teaching from the* Heart (1996).

Reginald D. Archambault: Author.

Hannah Arendt (1906–1975): German-American political theorist; Guggenheim fellow; professor at Princeton University; president of the University of Chicago; author of *Teaching as Leading* and *The Origins of Totalitarianism*.

Aristotle (384–322 B.C.): Greek philosopher who studied under Plato; proponent of logic.

Arthur Ashe (1943–1993): African-American tennis player and social activist; chairman of the American Heart Association; National Tennis Center stadium named in his honor after he died of AIDS-related pneumonia.

Sylvia Ashton-Warner (1905–1984): New Zealand novelist and educational philosopher; author of *Teacher*.

Isaac Asimov (1920–1992): Russian-American scientist and author of more than four hundred books.

Richard Bach (1936–): Author of *Jonathan Livingston Seagull, The Bridge Across Forever,* and *Illusions: The Adventures of a Reluctant Messiah.*

Francis Bacon (1561–1626): English knight, philosopher, and Parliamentarian.

James Baldwin (1924–1987): African-American expatriate, author, and preacher concerned with issues of race and homosexuality.

Hosea Ballou (1771–1853): Theologian who founded the Universalist Church and denied the concept of original sin.

Edward C. Banfield (1916–): U.S. political scientist.

Bernard Baruch (1870–1965): Stock market speculator, economist, and representative to the United Nations Atomic Energy Commission in 1946.

Jacques Barzun (1907–): French-American historian; teacher and dean at Columbia; one of the founders of the discipline of cultural history.

Melba Patillo Beals (1942–): One of a group of African-American students integrated into Little Rock schools; author of the autobiographical *Warriors Don't Cry.*

William J. Bennett: (1943–) United States secretary of education, national "drug czar," and author of *The Book of Virtues, The Children's Book of Virtues,* and *The Death of Outrage: Bill Clinton and the Assault on American Ideals.*

Claude Bernard (1813–1878): French physiologist; taught at Collège de France and Sorbonne; author of *An Introduction to the Study of Experimental Medicine.*

Leonard Bernstein (1918–1990): Musical director of New York Philharmonic-Symphony Orchestra; composer and conductor; professor at Brandeis University.

Arthur Bestor (1908–): American educator and historian.

William Blake (1757–1827): English poet, painter, engraver, and mystic.

Allan Bloom (1930–1992): American political scientist and writer.

Harold Bloom (1930–): literary scholar; professor at Yale University and New York University; author of *Stories and Poems for Exceptionally Intelligent Children of All Ages*, *How to Read and Why*, and *The Anxiety of Influence.*

Derek Bok (1930–): President at Harvard University (1971–1990); author of *Beyond the Ivory Tower*, *Higher Learning*, and *Universities and the Future of America.*

Daniel J. Boorstin (1930–): Pulitzer Prize–winning author of *The Americans*; Rhodes Scholar; director of the National Museum of American History and senior historian of Smithsonian Institution; professor of history at the University of Chicago.

Ernest L. Boyer (1928–1995): Chancellor of New York State University (1970–1976); United States commissioner of education (1977–1979); president of the Carnegie Foundation for the Advancement of Teaching (1979).

Kingman Brewster (1919–1988): President of Yale University; ambassador; pacifist.

Jacob Bronowski (1908–1974): Polish-born educator.

Henry Peter Brougham (1778–1868): British jurist and politician.

Jerome S. Bruner (1915–): American psychologist and author.

Buddha (563–483 B.C.?): Spiritual leader; born in Southern Nepal region; first tales told two hundred years after his death. "Four noble truths" and "eightfold path" describe his basic doctrine of Buddhism.

Warren E. Burger (1907–1995): Chief justice of the United States Supreme Court (1969–1986); called for programs to teach convicts how to read and write.

Sir Herbert Butterfield (1900–1979): English historian.

Helen Caldicott (1938–): Australian physician, peace activist, professor of pediatric medicine at Harvard, and author; founder of Physicians for Social Responsibility and Women's Action for Nuclear Disarmament.

George Carlin (1937–): Comedian; actor; author of *Brain Droppings* and *Napalm and Silly Putty*.

Marcus T. Cicero (106–43 B.C.): Roman orator, politician, and philosopher.

William Jefferson Clinton (1946–): Forty-second president of the United States (1993–2000); Rhodes Scholar; husband of New York State senator, Hillary Rodham Clinton.

Esmé Raji Codell: Latin-American teacher and language arts specialist; *Educating Esmé* is the story of her first year of teaching.

Joanna Cole (1944–): Author of science and nature books as well as the best-selling *Magic School Bus* series.

Marva Collins (1938–): American teacher and author.

John Amos Comenius (1592–1670): Bishop of the Moravian Church; advocated education that relates to everyday life as well as equal educational opportunities for women.

James Bryant Conant (1893–1978): President of Harvard University (1933–1953); chemist involved in the development of the atomic bomb.

Confucius (c. 551–479 B.C.?): Known for *Analects* (sayings that were collected by his disciples) and his desire for a stable government in China.

Pat Conroy (1945–): English teacher; author of *Prince of Tides, The Lords of Discipline,* and *Beach Music.*

Bill Cosby (1937–): Comedian; actor; author of *Fatherhood.*

George S. Counts (1889–1974): Professor of education at Columbia; president of the American Federation of Teachers; author of *The Prospects of American Democracy* and *Education and the Foundations of Human Freedom.*

Norman Cousins (1915–1990): Editor of *The Saturday Review;* overcame life-threatening illness and heart attack, which he wrote of in numerous inspirational books; received the United Nations Peace Medal.

Mihaly Csikszentmihalyi: Professor of psychology at the University of Chicago; author of *Flow: The Psychology of Optimal Experience.*

Marie Curie (1867–1934): French physicist who coined the term "radioactivity"; awarded the Nobel Prize twice; worked closely with her husband, Pierre, and her daughter, Irène.

Melitta J. Cutright: Author of *Growing Up Confident.*

John Cotton Dana (1856–1929): President of the Special Libraries Association and the American Library Association; author of *A Library Primer* and *The New Museum.*

Linda Darling-Hammond: Co-director of the National Center for Restructuring Education, Schools and Teaching; executive director of the National Commission on Teaching and America's Future; author of *The Right to Learn: A Blueprint for Creating Schools That Work.*

Clarence Darrow (1857–1938): Lawyer who defended a Tennessee teacher who taught the theory of evolution in the Scopes-Monkey trial.

René Descartes (1596–1650): French scientist, mathematician, and philosopher; helped usher in modern era of science and philosophy.

John Dewey (1859–1952): Philosopher, writer, and professor at the University of Chicago and Columbia University; argued against authoritarian educational methods and for reforms like women's suffrage.

Dorothy De Zouche: Teacher.

Charles Dickens (1812–1870): British novelist; author of *Oliver Twist, Great Expectations*, and *David Copperfield*.

John Sloan Dickey: President of Dartmouth College.

Walt Disney (1901–1966): Animator and movie producer.

Benjamin Disraeli (1804–1881): British prime minister and founder of modern Conservative party; author of *Vivian Grey, Coningsby*, and *Sybil*.

Frederick Douglass (c. 1817–1895): The foremost African-American abolitionist in ante-bellum America.

Alexandre Dumas (1802–1870): Self-educated author of *The Three Musketeers* and *The Count of Monte Cristo*.

Isadora Duncan (1878–1927): Innovative dancer who preferred to dance barefooted.

Will Durant (1885–1981): Historian and author of the eleven-volume collection, *The Story of Civilization*.

Ecclesiastes: Book of the Bible that was written by Solomon, around 300 B.C.; focused on futility of life and being a God-fearing person.

Meister Eckhart (1260–1328): 13th-century Dominican mystic.

Thomas A. Edison (1847–1931): Invented the phonograph, telegraph, and lightbulb; held over thirteen hundred patents; his Edison Electric Light Company became General Electric; believed in teamwork over individual accomplishment.

Mark Edmundson: Professor of English at the University of Virginia; contributing editor to *Harper's Magazine*; author of *Teacher* and *Nightmare on Main Street*.

Otis C. Edwards: Episcopal priest.

Albert Einstein (1879–1955): Physicist who developed the theory of relativity.

Elliot Eisner: High school art teacher; professor of education and art at Stanford University; author of *The Educational Imagination: On the Design and Evaluation of School Programs*.

George Eliot, pseudonym of Marian Evans (1819–1880): English author best known for her novel *Middlemarch*.

Ralph Waldo Emerson (1803–1882): Father of transcendentalism; mentor to Henry David Thoreau; author; minister.

Epictetus (c. 55–c. 130 A.D.): Stoic Greek philosopher; taught that true good is *within* oneself and to respond intelligently to one's own needs and duties.

Desiderius Erasmus, pseudonym of Gerrit Gerritszoon (1466–1536): Satirical Dutch writer; Catholic priest and professor of divinity often critical of the Church.

Euripides (480–406 B.C.): Greek writer of approximately ninety plays, including *The Bacchae*.

Mari Evans (1923–): Professor at Indiana and Purdue; playwright and author of *A Dark and Splendid Mass, Black Women Writers 1950–1980: A Critical Evaluation,* and *How We Speak*.

Chester E. Finn, Jr.: Professor of education at Vanderbilt University; John M. Olin Fellow at Manhattan Institute and president of the Thomas B. Fordham Foundation; founding partner of the Edison Project.

Malcolm S. Forbes (1919–1990): American publisher who became a multimillionaire.

Henry Ford (1863–1947): Father of the Ford Motor Company; pioneered the assembly line.

Max Forman: Special-education consultant, California Dept. of Education.

Anatole France, pseudonym of Jacques Anatole Thibault (1844–1924): French author awarded the Nobel Prize in literature in 1921.

Benjamin Franklin (1706–1790): Owner and printer of the *Pennsylvania Gazette* and *Poor Richard's Almanac*; established America's first lending library; conducted experiments with electricity; patriot and diplomat.

Ursula Franklin (1921–): Founder, Ursula Franklin Academy.

Sigmund Freud (1856–1939): Founder of psychoanalysis.

Robert Frost (1874–1963): Poet; schoolteacher and professor at Harvard University, Amherst University, and the University of Michigan.

Claude M. Fuess (1885–1965): American author and biographer.

Michael Fullan: Dean of the Ontario Institute for Studies in Education at the University of Toronto; author of *The New Meaning of Educational Change* and the *What's Worth Fighting For* series.

Mary Hatwood Futrell (1941–): Dean of George Washington University's School on Educational Leadership; president of Education International.

Galileo Galilei (1564–1642): Physicist; inventor of the telescope; was placed under house arrest during the Inquisition for supporting the Copernican claim that the sun is the center of the universe.

Indira Gandhi (1917–1984): First female prime minister of India (1966–1977, 1980–1984).

Mahatma Gandhi (1869–1948): Indian political and spiritual leader who impacted the civil rights movements worldwide.

David P. Gardner: President, University of Utah.

A. Bartlett Giamatti (1938–1989): President of Yale University (1978–1986) and of major league baseball's National League (1986–1989); commissioner of major league baseball (1989).

Khalil Gibran (1883–1931): Lebanese poet who wrote *The Prophet*.

Althea Gibson (1927–): First African-American woman to play in United States grass court championships at Forest Hills and at Wimbledon; member of the National Lawn Tennis Hall of Fame.

Virginia Gildersleeve (1877–1965): American educator, dean of Barnard College.

Henry A. Giroux (1943–): Social studies teacher; professor of secondary education at Miami of Ohio University and Penn State University; author of *Border Crossings, Pedagogy and the Politics of Hope,* and *Teachers as Intellectuals.*

Ellen Glasgow (1873–1945): Writer who rejected the interwoven code of Southern chivalry and male chauvinism; awarded the Pulitzer Prize for *In This Our Life.*

Gail Godwin (1937–): Author of *Heart: A Personal Journey through Its Myths and Meanings, Evensong, The Odd Woman,* and *A Mother and Two Daughters.*

Johann Wolfgang von Goethe (1749–1832): Scientist and poet synonymous with the German Romantic period; author of *Faust.*

John Goodlad: Director of the Center for Educational Renewal; professor at University of California at Los Angeles, the University of Chicago, and the University of Washington; author of over thirty education books.

Graham Greene (1904–1991): Author of short stories, plays, and his autobiography as well as several novels, including *The Power and the Glory* and *The End of the Affair.*

Kurt Hahn (1886–1974): German educationist.

Lord Haldane (1856–1928): British statesman and philosophical writer (*Pathway to Reality, Reign of Relativity,* and *The Philosophy of Humanism*).

Edith Hamilton (1867–1963): Headmistress at Bryn Mawr School

(1896–1922); author of *The Greek Way* and *Mythology*.

Andy Hargreaves: Director, Center for Educational Change, University of Toronto.

Nathaniel Hawthorne (1804–1864): Author of classic morality tales including *The Scarlet Letter*.

Helen Hayes (1900–1993): Actress who won Academy Awards for her roles in *The Sin of Madelon Claudet* and *Airport*.

Georg Hegel (1770–1831): German philosopher; Hegelian dialectic states that progress is rational (thesis leads to antithesis leads to synthesis).

Robert Heinlein (1907–1988): American author.

Sir Alan Herbert (1890–1971): English politician and author of *The House by the River, The Water Gypsies,* and *The Singing Swan.*

Theodore M. Hesburgh (1917–): Clergyman, president of Notre Dame University.

Jane Sequichie Hifler: Kindergarten teacher.

Gilbert Highet (1906–1978): Columbia University professor of Greek and Latin; author of *The Art of Teaching*; husband of novelist, Helen MacInnes.

Joel H. Hildebrand (1881–1983): Longtime professor of chemistry at Berkeley University; president of the Sierra Club (1940–1941).

Richard Hofstadter (1916–1970): American history professor at Columbia University (1946–1970), where he won Pulitzer Prizes for *The Age of Reform* and *Anti-Intellectualism in American Life.*

Oliver Wendell Holmes (1841–1935): Supreme Court justice (1902–1935) who established the "clear and present danger" rule in defense of First Amendment rights.

John Holt (1923–1985): American educational reformer who became a leader in the home-schooling movement.

Michael K. Hooker: Former chancellor, University of North Carolina, Chapel Hill.

bell hooks, pseudonym of Gloria Watkins (1952–): Professor at City College of New York; author of more than twenty socially conscious books, including *Killing Rage: Ending Racism, Outlaw Culture,* and *Teaching to Transgress: Education As the Practice of Freedom.*

Sam Houston (1793–1863): President of the Republic of Texas (1836–1838, 1841–1844) who opposed Texas secession from the Union.

Edgar Watson Howe (1853–1937): editor, essayist, and novelist.

Harold Howe II: United States commissioner of education (1965–1968); author of *Thinking about Our Kids* and *Barriers to Excellence.*

Elbert Hubbard (1856–1915): American writer and craft colonist.

Langston Hughes (1902–1967): African-American poet, novelist, and playwright of the Harlem Renaissance; author of "A Negro Speaks of Rivers," "A Dream Deferred," and the "Simple" stories.

Victor Hugo (1802–1885): French author of *Notre Dame de Paris* and *Les Misérables.*

Robert M. Hutchins (1899–1977): Professor and dean at Yale Law School; named president of the University of Chicago at age thirty (1945–1951); chairman of *Encyclopaedia Britannica*; founder of the Center for the Study of Democratic Institutions; author of *The Higher Learning in America* and *The University of Utopia.*

Thomas Huxley (1825–1895): English biologist and educator; advocate of Darwinism in England; author of *Evolution and Ethics.*

Lee Iacocca (1924–): Chairman of Chrysler Corporation (1978–1992); author of autobiographical *Iacocca.*

William Ralph Inge (1860–1954): English clergyman and theologian.

John Irving (1942–): Author of best-selling novels including *The World according to Garp, The Cider House Rules,* and *A Prayer for Owen Meany;* member of the Wrestling Hall of Fame.

Andrew Jackson (1767–1845): Seventh president of the United States (1829–1837); in favor of direct participation in government; known as "Old Hickory."

William James (1842–1910): Philosopher who taught at Harvard University; author of *Principles of Psychology.*

Thomas Jefferson (1743–1826): Third president of the United States (1800–1808); author of the *Declaration of Independence.*

David Johnson: Author of *The Social Psychology of Education.*

Kenneth G. Johnson: Paleontologist.

Lyndon B. Johnson (1908–1973): Thirty-sixth president of the United

States. (1963–1968); vice president under John F. Kennedy; proponent of Great Society reforms.

Thom Jones: American author.

James Joyce (1882–1941): Irish novelist; author of *Ulysses* and *Dubliners*.

Carl Jung (1875–1961): Swiss psychiatrist and founder of analytical psychology; contemporary of Freud; president of the International Psychoanalytic Society (1911–1914); developed the concept of extroversion and introversion.

Hannah Kahn (1911–1988): American author and poet.

Immanuel Kant (1724–1804): German philosopher; proposed that individuals' ideas do not have to conform to a common reality to be considered true.

Barnaby C. Keeney: President of Brown University and the National Endowment for the Humanities.

Helen Keller (1880–1968): Blind, deaf, and mute; author of *The Story of My Life, The World I Live In, Helen Keller's Journal, 1936–1937,* and *The Open Door.*

Thomas à Kempis (1379–1471): German religious writer.

George F. Kennan (1904–): Ambassador and professor of historical studies at Princeton University who won the Albert Einstein Peace Prize for efforts to improve United States–Soviet relations during the Cold War.

John F. Kennedy (1917–1963): Thirty-fifth president of the United

States (1961–1963); first Catholic president; his New Frontier legislation provided federal aid to schools and economically depressed areas; lent personal support to the civil rights movement.

Charles F. Kettering (1876–1958): Holder of three hundred patents, including the first electrical ignition system; founder of Dayton Engineering Laboratories Company (Delco); financed the Sloan-Kettering Institute for Cancer Research with Alfred Sloan.

Ellen Key (1849–1926): Swedish author who wrote *The Century of the Child*.

Soren Kierkegaard (1813–1855): Danish philosopher who saw truth as subjective; defended his existential dialectic by focusing on religious and aesthetic concepts.

James R. Killian (1904–1988): President, Massachusetts Institute of Technology.

Martin Luther King, Jr. (1929–1968): Minister, orator, and civil rights leader famous for his "I Have a Dream" speech; author of *Stride toward Freedom, Why We Can't Wait,* and *Where Do We Go from Here: Chaos or Community?*

Stephen King (1947–): Author of numerous short stories, screenplays, and books including *The Shining, Carrie, Misery, The Stand,* and the *Dark Tower* series.

Barbara Kingsolver (1955–): Science journalist and author of the novels *Animal Dreams, Prodigal Summer,* and *The Poisonwood Bible.*

Rudyard Kipling (1865–1936): Nobel Prize–winning author of the classic children's story, *The Jungle Book.*

Grayson Kirk (1903–1997): President of Columbia University.

Alfred Korzybski (1879–1950): Polish-American linguist who developed "General Semantics."

Jonathan Kozol (1936–): Best-selling author of several books including *Savage Inequalities* and *Illiterate America;* Rhodes Scholar.

Aung San Suu Kyi (1945–): Nobel Peace Prize winner in 1991 and leader of Burma's National League for Democracy.

Stephen Leacock (1869–1944): Canadian economist; head of political science and economics departments at McGill University; author of humorous works including *Literary Lapses, Nonsense Novels,* and *Frenzied Fiction.*

Eda LeShan (1922–2002): Children's advocate and author.

Leon Lessinger: Dean, College of Education, University of Southern California.

Paula Polk Lillard: Founder of Forest Bluff School (Montessori preschool); author of *Montessori: A Modern Approach* and *Montessori in the Classroom.*

Henry M. Levin: Professor of education, Stanford University.

Abraham Lincoln (1809–1865): Sixteenth president of the United States (1861–1865).

Ann Lieberman: Emeritus professor, Teachers College, Columbia University.

John Locke (1632–1704): Philosopher and founder of British empiricism; proponent of middle class's right to property.

John Lubbock (1834–1913): British archaeologist.

Martin Luther (1483–1546): German leader of the Protestant Reformation who publicized his "Ninety-five Theses" to protest the dispensation of indulgences.

Helen MacInnes (1907–1985): Spy novelist and author of more than twenty books; wife of educator, Gilbert Highet.

James Madison (1751–1836): Fourth president of the United States (1809–1817); wrote federalist papers with Alexander Hamilton and John Jay; advocated for the *Bill of Rights*.

Horace Mann (1796–1859): Educator and politician; professor of philosophy and theology at and president of Antioch College (1853–1899); highly critical of fascism.

Thomas Mann (1875–1955): German novelist.

Sybil Marshall (1913–): Primary school educator and author of educational texts as well as fiction.

Harriet Martineau (1802–1876): English writer.

Konosuke Matsushita (1894–1989): Self-made Japanese businessman who founded the Matsushita Electric Industrial Corporation; extolled in *Matsushita Leadership*.

Federico Mayor: Director of UNESCO (1987–1999); coauthor of *The World Ahead* and *Blue Geopolitics: The United Nations*

Reform and the Future of the Blue Helmets.

Benjamin E. Mays (1894–1984): President of Morehouse College (1940–1967); *Born to Rebel* is his autobiography; his biography is *Walking Integrity: Benjamin Elijah Mays, Mentor to Martin Luther King Jr.*

Christa McAuliffe (1948–1986): Science teacher chosen to be astronaut who died on the NASA space shuttle *Challenger.*

David O. McKay (1873–1970): Morman humanitarian and educator.

Margaret Mead (1901–1978): Anthropologist and writer; curator of ethnology for the American Museum of Natural History; adjunct professor of anthropology at Columbia University; early proponent of studying the perspectives of women and children.

Louis Mercier, French author and educator.

Michelangelo Buonarroti (1475–1564): Italian master of painting, sculpture, and architecture.

James A. Michener (1907–1997): Author of over a hundred books; private school teacher and college professor; sailor in the United States Navy during World War II.

Henry Miller (1891–1980): Author of the *Tropic of Cancer, Nexus,* and *The Air-Conditioned Nightmare*; advocated freedom from conventional restraints of civilization.

Wilson Mizner (1876–1933): Dramatist. Biographies are *Rogue's Progress: The Fabulous Adventures of Wilson Mizner* and *The Legendary Mizners.*

Ashley Montague (1905–1999): British-American anthropologist who taught at Graduate School of Medicine (New York University) and Rutgers; of the opinion that aggression is not natural to humans.

Thomas Moore (1779–1852): Irish poet.

Sir Claude Moser: Author, *The Miracle of the Beginning Reader.*

Muhammad (571?–634? A.D.): Orphan, preacher, warrior, emancipator, philosopher; the prophet of Islam, his name means "highly praised."

Ralph Nader (1934–): United States consumer advocate, author, and political reformer; lecturer in history and government at the University of Hartford; perennial Green Party candidate for president (1992, 1996, and 2000).

V. S. Naipaul (1932–) British author, born in Trinidad; chronicles difficulties of life in Third World; awarded the Nobel Prize for literature in 2001; knighted by Queen Elizabeth.

Patricia Neal (1926–): Oscar-winning actress for *Hud.*

C. B. Neblette: American teacher.

Nel Noddings: Professor of education, Stanford University.

Ewald B. Nyquist: New York State Commissioner of Education.

Vijaya Lakshmi Pandit (1900–1990): Indian diplomat; named first female president of the United Nations General Assembly in 1953; sister of Jawaharlal Nehru.

Dorothy Parker (1893–1967): Writer of poetry and satirical fiction; literary critic.

Norman Vincent Peale (1898–1993): Preacher; advocate for mental health services; author of *The Power of Positive Thinking.*

Johann Heinrich Pestalozzi (1746–1827): Swiss educational reformer who believed in treating children as individuals, that education should be moral *and* intellectual, and that society could be changed by education.

Jean Piaget (1896–1980): Swiss developmental psychologist; studied under Carl Jung; administered intelligence tests to children with Alfred Binet.

Plato (427?–347 B.C.): Greek teacher of math and philosophy; pupil of Socrates.

Alexander Pope (1688–1744): English poet; addressed social and political issues with satire.

Joseph Priestly (1733–1804): English theologian and scientist; his experiments with oxygen ("dephlogisticated air") were the foundation of modern chemistry.

Nathan M. Pusey (1907–2001): History professor at several colleges; president of Harvard University (1953–1971); author of *Age of the Scholar: Observations on Education in a Troubled Decade.*

Thomas Pynchon (1937–): Author of National Book Award winner, *Gravity's Rainbow.*

Anna Quindlen: Pulitzer Prize–winning (1992) journalist and author of *Object Lessons, One True Thing, Black and Blue,* and *Blessings.*

Quintilian (c. 35–c. 95 A.D.): Roman orator and teacher of rhetoric.

Sally Jessy Raphael (1943–): TV talk show host and radio personality.

John A. Rassias: Dartmouth College professor.

Dan Rather (1931–): Television journalist with CBS since 1962; author of six books.

Grantland Rice (1880–1954): Sports columnist, poet, magazine and book writer, film producer, and golfer. Read more in *How You Played the Game*.

Richard Riley (1933–): State representative, senator, and governor; United States secretary of education (1992–2000).

Tom Robbins, (1936–): Author of *Another Roadside Attraction* and *Even Cowgirls Get the Blues*.

Chris Robinson (1966–): Lead singer of The Black Crowes; husband of actress, Kate Hudson.

Fred "Mr. Rogers" Rogers (1928–): TV personality; parenting specialist.

Manley E. Rogers: Director of Admissions, U.S. Military Academy.

Will Rogers (1879–1935): American cowboy, entertainer, and humorist.

Andrew A. Rooney (1919–): Author of eleven books; columnist; has delivered his television essays on *60 Minutes* for the past twenty-four years

Mickey Rooney, pseudonym of Joe Yule, Jr. (1920–): Began acting as an infant and made over two hundred films; awarded an Oscar for lifetime achievement.

Theodore Roosevelt (1858–1919): Twenty-sixth president of the

United States (1901–1908); conservationist and author of several works of nonfiction including *Gouverneur Morris* and *Winning of the West*.

Leo Rosten (1909–1997): Celebrated Yiddish language and traditions; author of *The Education of Hyman Kaplan*.

Jean Jacques Rousseau (1712–1778): Swiss-French philosopher and author; refuted original sin, stating that humanity was good by nature and corrupted by civilization.

John Ruskin (1819–1900): Artistic critic and social theorist of nineteenth-century England.

Bertrand Russell (1872–1970): British philosopher, mathematician, and social reformer.

William Safire (1929–): American journalist and political columnist.

Jerome David "J. D." Salinger (1919–): Author of *The Catcher in the Rye* and the short story collection, *Franny and Zooey*.

George Santayana (1863–1952): Spanish-American philosopher and author of *The Last Puritan* and *His Dominations and Powers*.

George Savile (1633–1695): British educator.

Arthur Schopenhauer (1788–1860): German philosopher; stated that music was the best way to escape from pain; influenced Friedrich Nietzsche and Sigmund Freud.

Albert Schweitzer (1875–1965): Alsatian theologian, scientist, humanitarian, musician, and medical missionary; "reverence for life" describes his universal concept of ethics.

Pete Seeger (1919–): Songwriter, folk singer, and social activist.

Lucius Annaeus Seneca (c. 4 B.C.–65 A.D.): Spanish-born rhetorician who spent most of his life in Rome; author of *Controversies, Persuasions,* and a history of Rome.

Thomas J. Sergiovanni: Professor of education at Trinity University; senior fellow at the Center for Educational Leadership; author of *Building Community in Schools* and *The Principalship: A Reflective Practice Perspective.*

Dr. Seuss, pseudonym of Theodor Seuss Geisel (1904–1991): Author and illustrator of children's books including *The Cat in the Hat, Oh, the Places You Will* Go; and *The Grinch Who Stole Christmas.*

Albert Shanker (1928–1997): Executive director of the American Federation of Teachers (1974–1997); founder of the Albert Shanker Institute, dedicated to children's education as well as supporting unions as advocates for quality.

Svi Shapiro: Professor, University of North Carolina, Greensboro.

George Bernard Shaw (1856–1950): Irish playwright and critic; awarded the Nobel Prize in literature; author of *Pygmalion,* which later became *My Fair Lady.*

Shel Silverstein (1932–1999): American poet, cartoonist, and composer.

Georg Simmel (1858–1918): German philosopher and lecturer; contributed greatly to the establishment of German sociology as an independent discipline.

Alan Simpson (1931–): Conservative United States senator.

Ira Singer: Philosophy professor, Hofstra University.

Theodore R. Sizer: (1932–) Director of the Annenberg Institute for School Reform; professor of education at Brown University, where he created the Coalition of Essential Schools; author of *Horace's Compromise.*

B. F. Skinner (1904–1990): Psychologist and professor who was the leading proponent of behaviorism.

Thomas Sobol (1939–): Professor, Teachers College, Columbia University.

Socrates (469–399 B.C.): Greek philosopher who saw pursuit of philosophy as necessary for all intelligent men; teacher of Plato; originated the idea of "dialectic" (examining statements by pursuing their implications).

Herbert Spencer (1820–1903): English philosopher who said all phenomena are interpreted according to the principle of evolutionary progress; collaborated with Charles Darwin and Thomas Huxley on the theory of evolution.

Sir Richard Steele (1672–1729): British essayist, playwright, and politician.

Robert Louis Stevenson (1850–1994): Scottish writer handicapped by tuberculosis; author of *Treasure Island, Kidnapped,* and *The Strange Case of Dr. Jekyll and Mr. Hyde.*

Igor Stravinsky (1882–1971): Russian-American composer of the ballet *Le Sacre du Printemps (The Rite of Spring),* recognized as a masterpiece of modern music.

Anne Sullivan (1866–1936): Teacher and lifelong companion to Helen Keller; author and advocate for the deaf; portrayed in *The Miracle Worker*.

Charles Swindoll: Chancellor of Dallas Theological Seminary; author of twenty-plus books, including *Grace Awakening* and *Laugh Again*.

Thomas Szasz (1920–): Hungarian-American psychiatrist and author.

Stacia Tausher: American educator.

Mother Teresa, born Agnes Gonxha Bojaxhiu (1910-1997): Nurse and Nobel Prize–winning missionary who once worked as headmaster of a high school in Calcutta.

Henry David Thoreau (1817–1962): Writer and naturalist who fought against social conformity; author of *Walden* and "Civil Disobedience."

James Thurber (1894–1961): Humorous writer and cartoonist; *New Yorker* contributor who collaborated with E. B. White on the satirical *Is Sex Necessary?*

Ho Boon Tiong: Singapore educator.

Alvin Toffler: American author and futurist.

Jean Toomer (1894–1967): Writer and prominent figure in the Harlem Renaissance; author of *Cane*.

Arnold J. Toynbee (1889–1975): English historian.

Forrest "Frosty" Troy: Orator; defender of public education; editor of the *Oklahoma Observer*; author of the "You Want Heroes?" salute to teachers.

J. Lloyd Trump (1908–): Author of *Secondary School Curriculum Improvement: Proposals and Procedures* and *Focus on Change: Guide to Better Schools.*

Mark Twain, pseudonym of Samuel Langhorne Clemens (1835–1910): Author of numerous novels and short stories, including *The Adventures of Huckleberry Finn* and *The Adventures of Tom Sawyer.*

Mark Van Doren (1894–1973): Poet and critic; professor of English at Columbia University (1920–1959); author of *American and British Literature since 1890* and the play, *The Last Days of Lincoln.*

Henry Van Dyke (1852–1933): Clergyman, educator, and author who taught English literature at Princeton University; United States minister to the Netherlands.

Jules Verne (1828–1905): Founding father of modern science fiction and author of more than fifty books including *A Journey to the Center of the Earth, Twenty Thousand Leagues under the Sea,* and *Around the World in Eighty Days.*

Judith Viorst (1931–): American poet.

Swami Vivekananda (1863–1902): Hindu mystic and Vedanta philosopher who taught Hinduism in the United States.

Voltaire, pseudonym of Francois Marie Arouet (1694–1778): Enlightenment philosopher; author of *Candide,* in which he made his statement of practicality, "Let us cultivate our garden" (rather than contemplating the unanswerable questions).

William Arthur Ward: Author, *Truths for Living.*

Booker T. Washington (1856–1915): African-American educator who taught Native American students at Hampton University; directed Tuskegee Institute where he proposed that African-Americans needed economic equality before social equality could come.

Thomas Watson, Sr. (1874–1956): Founder of IBM; his son, Thomas Jr., helped lead the company to prominence.

Isabel Waxman: American educator.

Alfred North Whitehead (1861–1957): English mathematician, lecturer, and philosopher; taught at Cambridge University and Harvard University.

Walt Whitman (1819–1892): Poet who espoused virtues of individuality and democracy; some consider his self-published *Leaves of Grass* to be the most influential volume of poems in American history.

Ray L. Wilbur (1875–1949): Physician; professor; president of Stanford University (1916–1929, 1933–1943); United States secretary of the interior (1929–1933).

Oscar Wilde (1854–1900): Eccentric Irish writer of comedic stories and plays; imprisoned for purported homosexuality.

Oprah Winfrey (1954–): TV star known for *The Oprah Winfrey Show* as well as the Oprah Book Club; actress, writer, and film producer.

Alan Scott Winston: American author of *For the Love of Teaching.*

Thomas Wolfe (1900–1938): American writer and playwright.

Steven Wright (1955–): Comedian and actor.

William Yeats (1865–1939): Irish writer; revered for his poems "The Second Coming," "The Tower," and "Sailing to Byzantium."

Tom Yohe (1938–2001) American creator of the cartoon tutorial "Schoolhouse Rock."

Brigham Young (1801–1877): Shaped modern-day Mormonism; territorial governor of Utah after final westward move of his church.

Bibliography

Adler, Mortimer J. *The Paideia Proposal: An Educational Manifesto.* New York: MacMillan Publishing Co., 1982.

Albom, Mitch. *Tuesdays with Morrie.* New York: Doubleday, 1997.

Andrews, Robert, Mary Biggs, and Michael Seidel, et al. *The Columbia Encyclopedia.* Sixth Edition. New York: Columbia University Press, 2001.

Archambault, Reginald D. *John Dewey on Education.* Chicago: The University of Chicago Press, 1964.

Beals, Melba Patillo. *Warriors Don't Cry.* New York: Washington Square Press, 1994.

www.biography.com

Bloom, Harold. *Stories and Poems for Extremely Intelligent Children of All Ages.* New York: Scribner, 2001.

Brendtro, Larry, et al. *Reclaiming Youth at Risk: Our Hope for the Future.*

Carlin, George. *Napalm and Silly Putty.* New York: Hyperion, 2001.

Cosby, Bill. *Fatherhood.* Garden City, New York: Doubleday & Company, Inc., 1986.

Cutright, Melitta J. *The National PTA Talks to Parents: How to Get the Best Education for Your Child.* New York: Doubleday, 1989.

Dewey, John. *Philosophy of Education.* Totowa, New Jersey: Littlefield, Adams & Co., 1958.

www.ed.gov/pubs/FirstYear

www.ed.gov/pubs/survivalguide

Gross, Beatrice and Ronald. *The Great School Debate: Which Way for American Education.* New York: Simon & Schuster, Inc., 1985.

Gross, Ronald. *The Teacher and the Taught.* New York: Dell Publishing Co., 1963

Hargreaves, Andy and Michael Fullan. *What's Worth Fighting for Out There?* New York: Teachers College Press, 1998.

Highet, Gilbert. *The Immortal Profession.* New York: Weybright and Talley, 1976.

Kozol, Jonathan. *Illiterate America.* Garden City, New York: Anchor Press/Doubleday, 1985.

Johnston, Alva. *The Legendary Mizners.*

Kozol, Jonathan. *Savage Inequalities: Children in America's Schools.* New York: Crown Publishers, 1991.

Lillard, Paula Polk. *Montessori Today: A Comprehensive Approach to Education from Birth to Adulthood.* New York: Shocken Books, 1996.

A Nation at Risk: The Full Account.

Piaget, Jean. *Science of Education and the Psychology of the Child.* New York: Orion Press, 1970.

Sergiovanni, Thomas J. *Building Community in Schools.* San Francisco: Jossey-Bass Inc., 1994.

Simpson, James B. *Simpson's Contemporary Quotations.* Boston: Houghton Mifflin Company, 1988.

Sizer, Theodore R. *Horace's Compromise.* Boston: Houghton Mifflin, 1984.

Sizer, Theodore R. *Places for Learning, Places for Joy: Speculations on American School Reform.* Cambridge, Massachusetts, 1973.

I cannot join the space program and restart my life as
an astronaut,
but this opportunity to connect my abilities as an
educator
with my interests in history and space is a unique
opportunity
to fulfill my early fantasies.

Christa McAuliffe (1948–1986)

Index